HOW TO FIND A BETTER JOB

HOW TO FIND A BETTER JOB

BY JAMES NEYLAND

A GD/PERIGEE BOOK

Perigee Books
are published by
The Putnam Publishing Group
200 Madison Avenue
New York, New York 10016

Published simultaneously in Canada by General Publishing
Co. Limited, Toronto.
Library of Congress catalog card number: 80-83384
ISBN 0-399-50800-7
First Perigee printing, 1982
Two previous Grosset & Dunlap printings
Printed in the United States of America

Contents

Part I
The Résumé

1. No More Excuses! Write That Résumé

If you are reading this book, you are probably one of an increasing number of people in the United States who have an employment problem. You may also be approaching this book with some skepticism. Because your problem is distinctively your own, you may doubt that something as simple as a résumé can help you resolve it.

"After all," you may be telling yourself, "a résumé is nothing more than a list of qualifications and experience, no different from the job application forms I've been filling out. My problem is . . ."

And then you supply the specific reason for not having the job you want. Some of the most common are the following:

I'm entering the job market for the first time, and I have no experience.

My age is against me. (Either too young or too old.)

They keep telling me I'm overqualified or underqualified.

I didn't complete my education. (Either high school or college.)

The only employment I've had for the past ten years has been as wife and mother.

I've had plenty of experience, but it's all been in the wrong field.

I was fired from my last job, and when an employer asks me why I can't explain.

I'm a member of a minority group (black or Hispanic or other), *and employers are all prejudiced against me.*

I took two years off to bum around the country, and employers always take that to mean I'm unreliable.

I've gone as far as I can go in my line of work, and now it's a dead-end.

I've had too many different jobs in too few years; employers don't like that.

I've priced myself out of the job market.

I'm a misfit; I've tried one line of work after another, and still haven't found the right one.

The excuses—and they *are* excuses, rather than reasons—are legion. Any one of them will serve to keep you in your rut, either unemployed or unsatisfactorily employed.

If you accept your excuse as a reason for your situation, you have no one but yourself to blame. By accepting it, you will invariably convey it to prospective employers, and they will be looking for any reason not to hire you. As unfair as that may seem, you must remind yourself that employers almost invariably are faced with numerous applicants for a single job, and they must weigh both negative and positive qualities carefully to make the right choice. If you offer them negatives, you are helping them to discount you.

Some of you will resent that fact. If you like your misery, if you enjoy complaining about the injustice of the "System," close this book and go no further. You can get endless masochistic pleasure from being rejected time after time for jobs that only you know you are capable of doing.

If, however, you are genuinely interested in solving your employment problem, and if you are willing to acknowledge the way the employment system works, you can easily get the job you want.

What you must do is give the employer a reason to hire you. He will be looking for positive values in you as well as negative values. It is just as easy to offer him the qualities he is seeking as it is to present the qualities he does not want.

This does not mean that you should present your own personal reasons for applying for a position. An employer cannot be concerned about the fact that you have been out of work for six months, or that you have two children to support, or that you are unhappy in your present work. Although some might commiserate and offer you sympathy, few would offer you a job on that basis. In most cases, such a reason would actually work against you. An employer does not need your problems on top of his own; in fact, by hiring you, he is attempting to resolve some of his problems.

If you can convince an employer that this is precisely what he will do by hiring you, you will get the job. You must give him a reason to place his faith and trust in you, above all other applicants. You have something special to offer that no one else seems to have. That word "offer" is the key. When you apply for a job, you are not going begging, nor are you presenting yourself passively in the hopes that your merits will be recognized. You are selling a piece of merchandise—yourself, with all that entails, including your education, your experience, your contacts, and your special talents and abilities.

The most important part of your sales kit can be your résumé. It is the one piece of tangible evidence of who you are and what you are capable of doing. Often it precedes you, and it can be instrumental in getting you a personal interview, and usually—unless it has ended up in the "circular file," or wastebasket, which does frequently happen to weak and ineffective résumés—it remains with the employer as a reminder after your face-to-face opportunity has passed. Therefore, as your representative, it must be the most positive presentation you can make.

It must highlight all of your good qualities, minimize your weaknesses and emphasize the qualifications and experience that make you the right person for the job. It must do this clearly and concisely, so that a prospective employer will see at a glance that you are eminently qualified.

"But," you may protest, "an interviewer never really looks at a résumé. I always get asked the same questions that are written down on the piece of paper right in front of his eyes. So it doesn't really matter what's on that piece of paper."

In most cases, that is totally untrue. Some employers may appear not to look at résumés, but usually this appearance is only a technique of interviewing. A skilled interviewer will be thoroughly familiar with your résumé before meeting you, and will question you to determine how clearly you can express orally what you have written on paper. This is especially true with those résumés he is reviewing for his final choice.

No interviewer wants to spend lengthy time reading while you sit staring uncomfortably at him. Interview time is precious. An employer will want to spend every available moment assessing your manner, attitude, and personality traits, and so—if he has just received your résumé—he will simply glance at it for the salient points, and study it more carefully later.

If your résumé is properly done, a glance is all an interviewer will need. You will pique his interest immediately and he will be able to see that you are clear in your objectives, organized, efficient, and confident of your abilities.

With a poorly done résumé, he will be frustrated—perhaps even irritated—at having to waste precious time searching for the significant points, and that is not a good way to begin an interview.

2. Give the Employer What He Wants

Most people think of a résumé as a list of facts and dates that sum up one's education and work experience. They approach its preparation routinely, even carelessly, considering it a dull or annoying part of the job-hunting process. Invariably their attitudes are reflected in the résumés they produce. Most résumés are dull and uninteresting. Some are exasperating.

It is important to realize that an interviewer will get out of a résumé only what you put into it. If you put your boredom or annoyance into it, that's what he will get. If you put your energy, skill, and enthusiasm into it, you are certain to prompt a similar response.

Preparing your résumé should be a challenging and a creative process to be taken seriously. It is an integral part of career planning and job acquisition, and should not be done hastily or routinely. Do not simply update a résumé several years old or borrow someone else's résumé to use as a guide, unless your talents and qualifications are precisely the same.

The challenge lies in discovering precisely what an employer wants in an employee, and in determining precisely how you can give him what he wants. The creativity lies in making a single 8½-by-11-inch piece of paper convey that you are what he wants.

In applying for a job, it is important to remember that you are selling yourself. There is no point in protesting that you don't like the idea of presenting yourself as a piece of merchandise, or that you have talents and abilities any employer should recognize without your having to go out of your way to prove it. That attitude may enable you to maintain your pride and dignity, but it will not help you toward success. There is a system in American business and industry, and you must face the fact that you have to work within that system.

It is up to you to give the employer what he wants; unless you do, he is under no obligation to give you anything.

Specific jobs involve specific qualifications an employer will be looking for. If you are already employed in a field you will surely be aware of some of those qualifications, and you can probably determine the remainder without great difficulty by checking with friends and associates. If, however, you are setting out into the job market for the first time or after a long absence, or if you have decided to change fields, you will have to do a bit of research to learn what qualities a prospective employer will be looking for.

There are some qualities all employers will be looking for. Honesty, reliability, and truthfulness must be apparent on your résumé. While you can—and should—slant the facts on your résumé in your favor, you must avoid outright lies or inaccuracies. Lies will always catch up with you, whether or not you prove yourself capable of performing the job.

Another most important quality is a positive outlook. Often an employer will choose a cooperative applicant with lesser qualifications over a more qualified applicant whose attitude is negative or gloomy. Employees who are eager, energetic, even-tempered, and helpful are capable of learning what they do not already know. Employees who grumble, complain, and have difficulty getting along with others are likely to affect the attitudes of other employees by fostering a negative attitude throughout the company.

For that reason, it is imperative that you avoid negative comments. Do not talk about personality conflicts with your previous employers, nor describe petty rivalries among employees. If you must offer reasons for leaving previous jobs, make the reasons as positive as you can. Positive reasons include higher salary, need for advancement, expanding the scope of your work, desire to work for a larger (or smaller) company.

If you were fired from a previous job, and that firing did involve personality conflicts, try to avoid discussing them. Usually an employer will give more acceptable reasons when firing an employee—an economic cutback, a need for different skills, a change in the office structure. When those explanations exist, use them.

Other important qualities include punctuality, friendliness, the ability to listen and take orders, an objectivity about company rules and regulations, and a willingness to put the success of the business ahead of personal wishes. These may seem trite and old-fashioned, but they continue to apply to virtually all businesses and industries.

To some, these qualities may seem so obvious that there is no need to mention them. However, even the best of workers can easily lose sight of the important factors in their jobs and fall into the trap of negativism without realizing it. There are any number of factors on the job that can affect your mental attitude and cause you to lapse into bad work habits. If you don't correct these habits, they'll stand in your way while you look for a new job, and hinder your effectiveness after you find one.

3. Your Résumé Is a Learning Tool

Almost as important as what your résumé tells a prospective employer is what it can tell you about yourself. In the process of preparing your résumé you will find out a great many things you did not know—positive things as well as negative ones. Take advantage of those revelations—stress your positive attributes and minimize the negative—and you will be well on the way to getting the job that you want.

To accomplish this most effectively, it is helpful to write a preliminary résumé—one that is for your eyes only—before writing the final résumé that you will use as a sales tool. This preliminary résumé should break all the rules. It might be considered a lesson in how *not* to write a résumé. Write it in the first person, and be sure it describes all your achievements as well as all your mistakes. This preliminary résumé may run to several pages. It can be as long as you want. Once it has been completed and you have learned all you need to know about yourself as an employee, you may destroy it.

On pages 11–13, you will find examples of this type of résumé. One describes a woman reentering the job market after a fifteen-year absence; the other was written by a man who has been working steadily but has reached an impasse in his career. Both are capable of getting jobs that will be satisfying and profitable, but they also have problems that have to be dealt with at the résumé stage.

EXAMPLE I

JANE SMITH
0000 Elm Street
Pomona, California 90000
(213) 000-0000

JOB OBJECTIVE

After twenty years of drudgery and boredom as a housewife, I want to find a job that will be exciting, stimulating and challenging. I'll take anything if it pays moderately well and gets me out of the house to do something interesting involving other people. My wildest dream is to get into some field that is creative, using my talents in art, theater, and fashion.

WORK EXPERIENCE

For the past twenty years I've done nothing but manage a home for my husband and kids—three of them, with three impossibly different temperaments and personalities. In short, I've been a glorified servant, giving up everything I've always wanted so that my husband and children can have what they want. I've done everything that being a wife and mother entails. I've scrubbed toilets and floors; I've run a shuttle to schools and camps and movies; I've been a tutor in every academic subject there is; and, I've run the household budget.

I've been "interior decorator" on three separate residences, all our own homes. The first was done—literally—on a shoestring. The last—three years ago—had a decorating budget in high five figures. In all of them, I've entertained to help my husband succeed in his own career. In the process I've become highly skilled in giving cocktail parties and dinner parties, from the intimate to the enormous. I have become adept at seeing trouble coming in a group and warding it off before it ever becomes serious.

I've also had to mediate in quarrels among my own three children, and between them and their friends and schoolmates, not to mention trouble with other parents and schoolteachers. I haven't always met with the greatest of success, but sometimes I get despondent, feeling that I've wasted my life. All three kids have turned out pretty well, despite all the troubles, so I guess I've done a fairly good job.

Before I was married, I had only three years of real employment. From 1957 to 1960, I worked as secretary and administrative assistant to a swimsuit manufacturer. The job involved the usual typing, filing, dictation, and organizing of appointments—what used to be called "girl friday" stuff. The administrative assistant part of the job involved supervising the other secretaries' work, keeping tabs on the department heads to make sure they got their reports in on time, and coordinating the efforts of the public relations staff with the work done by the advertising agency. Although it was not my job specifically, on two occasions I ended up doing all the organizational work on water fashion shows, both of which were highly successful.

EDUCATION

From 1952 to 1956, I attended the University of California, where I received a Bachelor of Fine Arts degree. My major was Art History, though I took some courses in drawing, painting, and graphics as well. I was a fairly good student, though hardly at the top of my class. To be honest, I was much more interested in my social life and extracurricular activities than I was in my studies. I was president of my sorority as well as of several other clubs, including the Dramatic Society. During my last year, I was first runner-up in the campus beauty pageant, though you wouldn't know it to look at me now.

Since college I have taken a few courses at our local adult community college, but have not attempted to get an additional degree. I've taken a course in film, one in graphic design, one in creative writing (actually getting one piece of light verse published), and one in stage directing. That's a wide spectrum of subjects and reveals more of my wandering, indecisive mind than it does any coherence of purpose, but each one was undertaken with a specific purpose in mind. Mostly they related to my hobbies and my local club work.

Before college, I attended the Los Angeles public schools, grades one through twelve, graduating from high school with a high B average. It could have been an A average if I hadn't been so interested in the social activities. My greatest interest was in the Dramatic Club and in the high school paper, for which I was managing editor.

HOBBIES AND SOCIAL ACTIVITIES

Being a wife and mother has been a full-time, twenty-four-hour job, but over the years I have tried to take some time for myself just to preserve my sanity. My big love has been the local civic theater which I have managed for the past six years. I have appeared in a few productions and have directed a few others, but mostly I have managed and coordinated the program, keeping track of the finances and budget and presiding over the meetings of the theater committee. Of course, when you're involved with a community theater, you have to do a little bit of everything. I've designed and painted scenery, arranged for the advertising, and obtained all the supplies needed for the various productions.

Most of the other civic work I've done has been related to my being a wife and mother. I have been president of the school PTA on three separate occasions and at three different schools. I have done volunteer work at a local hospital, and have been involved in fund-raising drives for charity and for the local public television station. I have also served on various church committees.

EXAMPLE II

THOMAS SMITH
0000 St. John's Place
New York, N.Y. 10000
(212) 000-0000

JOB OBJECTIVE

I would like to find a job as a copy editor where I will be left alone to do my job, without unnecessary interference. I'm sick and tired of having to play politics in order to keep my job, and I would like to find a company that expects nothing more than my efforts and skills.

WORK EXPERIENCE

I am currently working at the Power Publishing Company, where I have been employed as a copy editor for the past two years. I am one of six copy editors, and by far the best. I am meticulous in my work, but in recent months I have not been doing my best because of the girl in the next cubicle who spends most of her day either talking on the phone to her boyfriend, or entertaining her office clique. I have complained to the managing editor, but it has done no good. He just doesn't like me. He defends the other copy editor, even though she hardly ever gets her work done on time.

For the preceding two years, 1976 to 1978, I was a copy editor at Cardinal Publications. The situation there was almost as bad as at Power. I was constantly having to work late and take manuscripts home, handling a far heavier work load than any of the other copy editors. However, my efforts were never appreciated. One of the editors had it in for me because I was constantly correcting her grammar and spelling when she made changes in an author's wording. In my opinion, a copy editor should correct mistakes, no matter who makes them. Eventually, I was fired from Cardinal and I'm sure the editor was responsible.

From 1974 to 1976, I was employed at Mulberry Books. My title was production editor, but the job was basically that of a copy editor. My responsibilities included seeing the manuscripts through production—proofreading galleys, slugging page proofs, checking camera copy and blues. I liked working at Mulberry very much, but I couldn't put up with my boss, the production manager. He was a drunk, pleasant and helpful in the mornings, but a raving lunatic after returning from lunch. Somehow he always seemed to pick on me.

My first job, from 1972 to 1974, was as an editorial trainee at Hart-Johnson Publishing.

EDUCATION

I have a master's degree in English from Wiley University in Ohio. My B.A. is from the University of Smithville, though I attended Jackson College the first two years. I am a Phi Beta Kappa and a member of Mensa. My grades were always among the highest in my class.

I attended the public schools of Jones City, Ohio, from 1954 to 1965, finished all twelve grades in ten years and graduated as class valedictorian.

Both of these applicants need the objectivity that can be provided by writing a bad résumé. Although the second example presented a much more serious employment problem, both Jane Smith and Thomas Smith were able to see themselves as prospective employers might see them. Their weaknesses far over-shadowed their positive qualities. The experience of writing these bad résumés has taught both what to avoid, not only in the writing of their final résumé, but in their job interviews as well.

Of the two, Jane Smith has less to overcome before getting the job she wants. For those who automatically assume that a woman going back to work after a long absence will have a difficult time, this may come as a surprise. Many women do have to struggle to make that big step, but others do not. Much depends on skills, but even more depends on attitude. Jane Smith had the same fear and insecurity that anyone might have after an absence from the job market. It showed in her résumé. However, after objectively reading her résumé, she saw that her talents outweighed her weaknesses. Jane Smith may have been out of the job market for twenty years, but she never stopped working or acquiring skills and knowledge. She did not realize this herself until she wrote the confessional résumé. She also recognized that one of her greatest assets was a positive attitude. To get the job she wanted, all she had to do was to focus on her skills and objectives.

Thomas Smith's task was more complicated. Although he was employed for the past eight years and was out of work only for a period of two weeks between jobs, he found himself being turned down by one employer after another. After he performed this exercise, he realized how prospective employers were seeing him. He had fallen into two very bad work habits. Without knowing it, he had been communicating a poor attitude in his résumé and during his interviews.

Thomas Smith had become a chronic complainer, perhaps not without justification, but this affected everyone around him. Although he was never entirely at fault, he was unable to see that he was even partially at fault until he began to analyze his confessional résumé.

The first thing he noticed was the recurring two-year pattern of his job changes. In eight years of employment, he held four different positions with four different employers, and never stayed at one job for more than two years. This pattern extended even to his college years. When he realized this, he was forced to ask himself why. The answer was complex and required much soul-searching.

Thomas Smith is a skilled and conscientious worker, the kind of employee any employer would want. However, he chose his line of work because he is also rather shy and inclined toward the solitary life. Like most shy people, he is sensitive about the approval or disapproval of others.

Very early in his career, he suffered what might be termed a "job trauma." In his second position, he worked for an erratic, temperamental boss with a drinking problem. Because of his sensitivity and his desire to please, Thomas Smith took this bad experience personally. After that, wherever he worked, he began to expect trouble. Within the first two years at each company, he invariably found it.

Without his realizing it, Thomas Smith already had the job he wanted. Prospective employers who interviewed him recognized that fact, and they knew they could not expect him to be a permanent employee. In two years, he would be out looking for another job, leaving behind a mood of dissension and disunity among the other employees.

In order to change his work pattern, Thomas Smith decided to remain at the Power Publishing Company and gave himself another year to resolve his problems. Realizing that his only dissatisfaction was caused by the disturbances coming from the next cubicle, he decided to approach his managing editor in an open and tactful manner. As a result, his cubicle was changed and he became much more pleasant in his overall manner.

Jane Smith and Thomas Smith exemplify only two of many employment problems. Your own problems may seem far removed from those discussed here. However, the same techniques apply. Once you have recognized and analyzed your problem, you are halfway toward solving it.

Step 1: Sit down and write your own confessional résumé. Express everything you think and feel about your job objective, your skills, employment record, education, and hobbies. Don't be afraid to write anything because no one will see it but you. Include all your complaints as well as your achievements.

Step 2: When you feel you have accomplished step one, read through what you have written. Use a red pen or pencil to underline every negative comment you've made. Circle every "I" you have used. Don't hedge. You're trying to be honest with yourself. Underline anything that seems to be a complaint or derogatory remark about anyone else.

Step 3: When you have finished reading and marking your confessional résumé with red, count the number of "I's" and the number of sentences you've used. If the number of "I's" is around half the number of sentences, you are relatively objective. If you have used as many (or more) "I's" as sentences, you are going to have to apply yourself in order to acquire the necessary objectivity.

Step 4: Consider each of the negative comments underlined in red. They are important problems you have to overcome. Analyze them to determine if they are problems you may have created or contributed toward. Ask yourself if you could have resolved them before, or if they can be resolved now. Use the margins to make comments and identify each as a complaint, insecurity, or cynical attitude.

One way or another, you must overcome these faults before you write your final résumé or go for an interview.

Step 5: Read through the résumé again, this time with a blue pen or pencil. Look for everything positive you have to say about yourself. Underline all special skills and attributes that would be beneficial to an employer. Don't apply this to only the job objective and employment record portions of your résumé. It was under hobbies that Jane Smith found many of her qualifications for a job as assistant to a producer of television commercials. Even if you are relatively objective about yourself, you may have talents and skills you have never acknowledged.

Step 6: Analyze each of the positive aspects as you did the negative; but this time, try to relate each to your job objective. Which attributes will help to qualify you for the job you want? Circle these in blue, or make a note of them in the margins, because these are the qualities you are going to emphasize in writing your final résumé. It will help if you can number them in order of importance to the job.

If you have difficulty following this procedure on your own résumé, go back to the examples of Jane Smith and Thomas Smith and mark up their résumés as instructed. By analyzing their positive and negative qualities, you may gain the necessary objectivity for your own.

4. How to Write a Résumé

As you may have perceived by now, your résumé serves two very important functions—to clarify your goals and assets in your own mind, and to present those goals and assets to a prospective employer. These two functions should always be kept in mind while preparing your final résumé. *Remember: If you are clear about what you want and what you can offer, you will be helping a prospective employer to hire you.*

Don't be too hasty about getting your résumé into its final form. Even if you have made important discoveries about yourself by writing the confessional résumé, you may still be able to discover more. Take the procedure step by step, and allow yourself enough time to consider all your limitless possibilities.

Generally, résumés follow a standard format. (See Example III on page 18.) There is a reason for this. Whatever type of employment you seek, you will be expected to conform to rules and regulations. The appearance of your résumé indicates how well you can do this. Slight variations will show ingenuity, initiative, resourcefulness, and creativity. Excessive and inappropriate variations—such as drawings or cute type—will be evidence that you are a misfit and unable to take your responsibilities seriously. If your variations are not made with a clear and obvious reason, you will be conveying that you are either ignorant or careless.

How much variation you use on your résumé will depend upon the kind of job you are seeking. If the job requirements are rigid and precise—for example, accountant, bookkeeper, secretary, computer programmer, physician, printer, schoolteacher—keep strictly to the standard résumé format. For jobs that require flexibility or ingenuity—such as social worker, editor, writer, advertising director, salesperson, or researcher—you may vary the résumé as long as the variation has a clear purpose.

There are certain minor variations in résumé formats that are useful if you have weaknesses you wish to minimize. (See "Dealing with Your Résumé Problems," page 44.)

The standard résumé includes eight categories presented in the following order: (1) Identifying Data, (2) Job Objective, (3) Work Experience or Skills, (4) Military Record, (5) Education, (6) Professional Affiliations, (7) Personal Data, (8) References. However, it is rare that all eight categories appear on a single résumé. Those most often left off (because they do not apply) are Military Record and Professional Affiliations. Generally, specific references are excluded as well, and there is a single line at the bottom of the page stating, "References supplied upon request." Sometimes the Job Objective heading is also omitted. The remaining four categories comprise the heart of the résumé and should always be covered in one form or another.

To determine which categories you will include on your résumé—and how you will include them—consider the function of each.

Identifying Data

It should be obvious that you have to provide your name, address, and phone number on your résumé: The employer has to know the name of the applicant and how to reach him or her. However, many job-seekers fail to realize why this information should come first on their résumés. They assume they will attract attention by having a "different-looking résumé," and so they place this information at the bottom of the page. This annoying practice is likely to prompt a prospective employer to toss the résumé in the wastebasket.

Your identifying data should be as clear as possible so that an employer will know immediately which applicant he is considering and how he can reach that applicant. Ideally, this information is centered at the top of the page, with your name typed entirely in capital letters. It should appear in the following form:

SIDNEY JONES
3124 Elm Street
Smithtown, Oregon 00000
(000) 123-4567

You may vary the placement of this information only under one circumstance. If including your personal data is the only thing that prevents you from fitting the résumé onto one page, to save space you may place the identifying data in the top left corner, and put the personal data in the top right-hand corner.

There is also only one variation permissible in the information you include with the identifying data. Think carefully before adding it. You may use both your home phone number and the phone number at your place of employment, but only if you normally receive a great many outside phone calls.

Job Objective

The job objective should always be a brief single statement written in clear and concise language. Because it appears at the very beginning of the résumé, it is the first impression that you, the applicant, will give to a prospective employer. Long convoluted sentences filled with ambiguous words and ambitious phrases will suggest that you are either a dreamer or uncertain about precisely what you want. If you have any doubts about the wording, use a simple straightforward statement, such as:

Position as editor of children's books.

Of course, that tells the prospective employer nothing more than the obvious. He will have to look elsewhere on the résumé to determine if you have the special qualities he's looking for. Ideally, the job objective should state that you are just the person that the employer is looking for—but you have to know precisely what the employer wants in order to do that.

For example, the applicant for the position of children's book editor may have heard of a specific job opening. She knows someone at the company, and so she calls to find out what sort of person they are looking for. She learns that the company is expanding and seeking new lines of books for children. That is perfect for her; she has some ideas for precisely what the publisher wants. Therefore, she states her job objective as follows:

Experienced children's book editor seeking position with publisher willing to try new ideas.

The moment the prospective employer reads that, he's interested. This applicant is precisely what he's been looking for and he's anxious to hear her "new ideas."

Of course, this assumes you are able to tailor your résumé for each prospective employer. This last stated job objective would not get the applicant a job with a publisher making economic cutbacks or one seeking a person to take over a series of books created by a previous editor. The only kind of job that résumé will get is one "with a publisher willing to try new ideas."

So choose your wording very carefully.

First, ask yourself precisely what sort of job you really want. Then, ask yourself if you are willing to limit your prospects to only that description. It is time-consuming to alter your job objective for each job application, but sometimes it is worth it. In most cases, it's best to make a simple statement. Save your selling points for the section on employment skills and experience.

It should be noted that there is a difference between job objective and career objective. Often young applicants—those just setting out into the job market for the first time—don't perceive the distinction and make the mistake of giving a career objective on a résumé. Except for a few special fields—such as the medical or legal professions or in scientific research—that information is best kept to yourself.

Most employers do not wish to be concerned about your career objective. If you seem to be overly interested in how quickly you can reach a higher-level job, you will arouse an employer's suspicions. The job may be simply a steppingstone in a career to you, but it is an important part of the employer's business. He wants to know if you will fit into his business and perform the job.

Work Experience or Skills

This is the most important part of your résumé. It is well worth the greatest time and effort to make sure it describes you properly and conveys all your experience and capabilities. Again, brevity is important, so choose your words carefully; make every word count.

EXAMPLE III

CONSTANCE SMITH
2222 Twin Oaks Blvd.
Apple Springs, Oregon 00000
(111) 111-1111

JOB OBJECTIVE

Supervisory position with medium-sized library.

WORK EXPERIENCE

1977–Present	Chief Librarian, Apple Springs Library. Managed staff of three; arranged programming for both adults and children; ordered all books and library materials; devised plan to extend library services to day care centers and nursing homes.
1975–1977	Assistant Librarian, Apple Springs Library. Worked with Chief Librarian in revising cataloging procedures; given responsibility for creating special programs for children.
1972–1975	Library Assistant (Part Time), Bayberry College Library, Bayberry, Oregon. Worked in school library while attending college, studying Library Science. Duties included ordering books and revising card catalog.

EDUCATION

1969–1972	Graduate School, Bayberry College, Master of Library Science.
1964–1969	Bayberry College, Bachelor of Arts, English.
1952–1964	Apple Springs Public Schools, Apple Springs, Oregon.

PROFESSIONAL ASSOCIATIONS

Member, American Library Association.

PERSONAL

Born: May 9, 1946, Apple Springs, Oregon
Status: Single
Health: Excellent

References Supplied Upon Request

Follow the standard format for listing your employment record. It will permit you to present yourself to your best advantage. A prospective employer will expect to see this format when he looks at your résumé, and any variation will take him by surprise. That surprise can work either to your advantage or disadvantage, depending upon the manner and degree of variation. (Excessive variation will surely work to your disadvantage, unless—as will be described later—you are someone entering the job market for the first time, or someone re-entering after a long absence.)

At the same time, however, you should be aware that the standard format is designed to work in favor of the employer, enabling him to perceive at a glance any weaknesses an applicant might have. Anyone who has not had steady, uninterrupted employment for at least ten years, or anyone who has had more than three jobs within a ten-year period without a logical increase in responsibility, is at a disadvantage.

The standard format calls for a straightforward listing of jobs held, in reverse chronological order. Generally, the job listings are set in two columns—a narrow column at the left indicates the dates for each position and a wider column at the right indicates position held, name of employer, and responsibilities and skills employed in each job. The job title is usually set off typographically in some way; it may be either underlined or typed entirely in capital letters so the interviewer can see your entire history at a glance. (See Example III, page 18.)

For some, the problem with this format is that the dates are displayed too prominently. If you have had interruptions in your career, periods when you were not working, this is going to show up glaringly. In some fields of work, your age may make a difference, and the dates will clearly show if you are approaching the age when most companies like to retire employees. Frequent job changing will also show up.

If the dates are more of a handicap than a help on your résumé, dispense with the column, or use it for displaying other information that will present you to better advantage. If the positions you have held are impressive, use the left column to call attention to them. The dates of employment then can be placed inconspicuously with the information in the right column. (See Example IV, page 20.)

In some cases, where your jobs have been widely varied, yet each job has contributed something special to your capabilities, you might wish to display your skills in the left column, but do this only if you wish to call attention to these skills. This alternative was considered by the housewife returning to work after twenty years (Example I), but she decided it was too limiting.

If there is nothing special you wish to call attention to you may dispense with the left column entirely and have all the necessary information in a single column of paragraphs. This format is particularly appropriate for someone who has held only one job, or whose jobs have all been more or less the same.

These are all acceptable variations within the standard format. None of them will be frowned upon by a prospective employer or interviewer; none will arouse undue suspicion that you may be trying to mislead or slant things in your favor.

The more extreme variations are recommended only for those who have serious job handicaps, or those who have nothing to lose by breaking away from the form. Just such a case is the housewife in Example I—a woman who had only one regular job, and that was twenty years ago. Another case would be a young person, just graduated from high school or college, who has never held a job of any kind. A person who wishes to make a drastic change in career would be another.

EXAMPLE IV

DAVID SMITH
1001 South Travelers Street
Chicago, Illinois 00000
(111) 111-1111

JOB OBJECTIVE

Sales position.

WORK EXPERIENCE

Sales Representative   GREAT LAKES QUALITY TOOLS, Chicago, Illinois. Responsible for selling merchandise to retail hardware stores, traveling throughout the Great Lakes area, developing new outlets. (1978–Present)

Sales Representative   CYCLE-MANIA, St. Louis, Missouri. Responsible for promoting and selling bicycles, tricycles, unicycles, and a variety of cycle products throughout the country. (1976–1978)

Customer Service Representative   DOUBLE DOLLAR CREDIT UNION, Los Angeles, California. Responsible for hearing customer complaints and routing them to staff of six for resolution. Involved extensive telephone contact with the public. (1972–1974)

EDUCATION

B.A., Sociology, University of California at Los Angeles, 1971.

Whiteside Public Schools, Whiteside, California, 1954–1966.

PERSONAL

Born: July 19, 1948, Whiteside, California
Height: 5′ 11″
Weight: 160 lbs.
Status: Married, 1 child
Health: Excellent

REFERENCES

Supplied upon request

These are all applicants who are basically untried in their chosen line of work, and they are asking an employer to take a chance by hiring them. In all cases, it will take an uncommon employer to offer them a job, and so it is not out of order for them to construct uncommon résumés.

If you have a similar problem, you may wish to replace the section on employment with a section devoted to skills, special talents, or personal qualities. If you do choose to follow this approach, it is most important for you to prepare yourself by doing the confessional résumé first so that you will be well aware of your assets.

Remember: A prospective employer reads a résumé to find evidence that you can perform a job. If you are lacking evidence (a job record), you must find some way of substantiating your claims for potential. You may not have held a position similar to the one you are trying to get, but the interviewer must have some basis for believing you can do the work. What experience—work, education, or hobby—impels you to try this line of work? What assures you that you can do it? If you can convince yourself, you will probably be able to convince an employer.

For example, a young man right out of high school wants to get a job as an automotive mechanic. Although he has never held a job, he knows he can do the work. Not only has he taken a course in auto repair in the school shop, but he has also done considerable work on his own car, as well as the cars of his friends and family. He made a list of the kinds of repair jobs he did. The list was a good one, and he was able to divide it into two columns, under the head-

ing of Automotive Skills. In the left column, he listed the parts of the car he worked on—transmission, brakes, radiator, wiring, etc. In the right column, he described the kinds of repair jobs he has done, including the make and model of car, and the results.

This young man also has certain personal characteristics that would make him a good employee. He listed these as well—"willing to learn, congenial, well-mannered, capable of taking orders and instructions." (See Example V, page 22.)

Jane Smith, in Example I, page 11, followed a similar course in putting together her final résumé. She realized that she had a great deal of talent and experience, even though little of it had been proven in a regular job. But she could give specific examples where she had demonstrated her ability. Her final résumé can be seen in Example VI on page 23.

An applicant who is trying to make a major change in career from one line of work to another will have the greatest difficulty of all. He will have to minimize his work experience while maximizing his potential. If many of the same skills are used in both jobs, he may not meet with resistance, but if they are totally different, he will. The rules set forth above still apply, but he must be prepared to face the question: "Why do you want to change?" To avoid the inevitable skepticism, it may be advisable to try to turn a handicap into an advantage by setting forth his reasons in the Job Objective statement, or dividing this section into two parts, placing a category of Special Talents ahead of the listing of Work Experience. This would show that he has been employed in the wrong line of work.

EXAMPLE V

BART JONES
123 North Tune Street
Tune City, Texas 70000
(222) 222-2222

JOB OBJECTIVE

Position as Automotive Mechanic.

AUTOMOTIVE SKILLS

Motor
Tuned up motor and bored cylinders on 1963 Buick LeSabre.

Transmission
Overhauled transmission on 1972 Chevrolet Impala.

Carburetor
Overhauled carburetor on 1963 Buick LeSabre.

Brakes & Shocks
Changed master cylinder on 1963 Buick LeSabre, and bled brakes. Replaced brake pads on disc brakes and installed new shocks on 1974 Toyota Corona.

Wiring
Repaired wiring on wipers, lights, and radio on 1963 Buick La Sabre.

Body Work
Straightened front fender on 1963 Buick LaSabre and repainted.

PERSONALITY TRAITS

Willing to learn—Congenial—Well-mannered—Capable of taking orders and instructions

---

EDUCATION

Graduated 1980 from Tune City High School, with a B average, after attending grades 1 through 12 in the Tune City public schools. Took all manual arts courses offered in high school, but was especially interested in automotive repair and metal-working, in both of which maintained a Grade of A.

PERSONAL

Born: September 9, 1962, Tune City, Texas
Height: 5' 10"
Weight: 155 lbs.
Status: Single
Health: Excellent

EXAMPLE VI

JANE SMITH
0000 Elm Street
Pomona, California 90000
(213) 000-0000

OBJECTIVE

Opportunity for creative challenge. Open to anything.

SKILLS		EXPERIENCE
Organizing	•	Arranged fashion shows, I.J. Thomas Swimwear, as part of job as administrative assistant to I. J. Thomas, 1957–1960. Wrote scripts for "Cocktails on the Beach" and "It's Cruise Time."
Managing	•	
Scheduling	•	Managed Pomona Civic Theater, 1974–1980. Responsible for schedules, budgets, advertising, promotion, designing programs. On six occasions also directed productions.
Directing	•	
Budgeting	•	Decorated three different homes in three distinctive styles on budgets—Modern, Early American, and French Provincial.
Designing	•	Entertained extensively.
Decorating	•	
Problem-solving	•	

HONORS AND ACTIVITIES

First Runner-up, Miss University of California, 1955
President, Mu Mu Mu Sorority, 1955–1956
President PTA, 1966, 1969, 1976
Hospital volunteer work, fund-raising for charity & Station KKKK

EDUCATION

B.F.A., 1956, University of California; majored in Art.

Courses in film, design, writing, and stage directing, Pomona Community College, 1974–1979.

PERSONAL

Born: December 20, 1934, Los Angeles, California
Status: Married, three grown children
Health: Excellent
Attitude: Eager to work, willing to learn and try new things, able to get along with anyone, not afraid to do the most menial task or to attempt the most difficult.

References supplied upon request.

Military Record

Anyone who has served in the military should include that fact on his or her résumé. In most cases, a simple statement of branch, rank, and satisfactory discharge will suffice, especially for those who have been out of the military for some time and have plenty of job experience as proof of ability.

In other cases, more information would be useful. If your service provided you with education, special skills, or experience that help you to qualify for the job you are seeking, you should take advantage of that fact. If military service is the only work experience you've had, you should actually highlight the information, possibly even placing it under the heading of Skills or Job Experience, following the pattern set forth above. (Many interviewers do have a tendency to skip over the military service record routinely.)

Education

The amount of space you give to your education will depend upon the amount of experience you have had since. If you have been in the work force for a number of years you will probably want to do no more than list the schools you attended in reverse chronological order, giving the years attended and the degree attained. In such cases, your education is looked upon as a part of your potential, and your work experience has to serve as the proof of that potential.

However, if you have a little or no work experience, your educational background can be an important part of your "selling" résumé. Treat your education as you would the employment or skills section, highlighting the aspects that are particularly important for the job you are seeking. Have you taken specialized courses that are applicable? What extracurricular activities have you been involved in? Did any of them show evidence of initiative, leadership, or particular skills?

For a college student, often the extracurricular activities can be more impressive than the grade-point average or the degree attained. The official college record shows only a student's ability to study and pass courses; the extracurricular activities show his ability to deal on a pragmatic level. For example, a journalism student who has been editor of the school paper will have had actual experience meeting newspaper deadlines. A law student who serves on the student court shows that he can deal on more than a theoretical level.

A student who has worked to pay his way through college shows a prospective employer even more. Working for an education shows determination, initiative, practicality, and resourcefulness. A person who can deal with the problems of working and studying at the same time is a valuable employee in any line of work.

An example for the résumé of a student just out of college can be seen on page 25.

Professional Affiliations or Hobbies

This division of the résumé provides you with an opportunity to include pertinent information on job capabilities which do not fit into the standard listing of experience or education. Some jobs and most professions are related to organizations or associations, and in such cases your membership should be noted. For example, a doctor or nurse would mention membership in medical associations; a lawyer would include bar associations; a librarian would give a listing of library organizations. For any job that requires membership in a union, you should, of course, state your membership. For a schoolteacher, both union and professional associations should be included. Any offices you have held in unions or organizations should also be mentioned.

A section on hobbies is pertinent only if your hobbies relate to your job, and show special skills or interests that are useful. For example, a knowledge of photography is helpful for someone seeking work in a camera shop, on the staff of a magazine, or in advertising or public relations. For some executive jobs, where work and social life meet, your ability to play golf or tennis may influence an employer's decision to hire you.

How you spend your spare time reveals much about you. Consider carefully before you

EXAMPLE VII

ERIC JONES
1234 Morgan Street
Morgan, Mississippi 00000
(222) 222-2222

JOB OBJECTIVE

Starting position as writer with city newspaper.

EXPERIENCE

Editor-in-Chief, 1979–80

Feature Editor, 1978–79

Sports Reporter, 1977–78

Reporter, 1976–77

The Daily Clarion, student newspaper at Morgan College, as part of the training for journalism students. It was a full-sized 16-page paper, published five days a week, supported entirely by advertising and sales and subscriptions.

For three years, 1973–1976, worked on staff of high school newspaper, The Morgan Messenger; editor-in-chief during senior year, 1975–76.

JOBS

1976–1977—The SUB Restaurant, worked weekends as waiter.

1977–1978—Morgan College Registrar's Office, worked part-time as clerk.

EDUCATION

B.A., Morgan College, 1980; major in Journalism, minor in History. Graduated in top ten percent of class of 2200.

Morgan Public Schools, 1964–1976.

HONORS AND EXTRACURRICULAR ACTIVITIES

Member Sigma Delta Chi, Journalism fraternity
Phi Beta Kappa
Outstanding Student Award, 1980
Member Student Council, 1977–1980

PERSONAL

Born: February 19, 1958, Morgan, Mississippi
Status: Single
Health: Excellent

References furnished on request.

share this information with a prospective employer. If you feel it will help you to get the job, by all means include your hobbies. But if you feel a prospective employer might view your hobbies unfavorably, leave this section out.

Personal Data

Your résumé should not show any reticence to reveal the personal information an employer is entitled to know. However, you should not offer too much. The minimum data to include are date and place of birth, marital status and number of children, if any, and the condition of your health. A simple, straightforward presentation is all that is necessary:

> Date and place of birth: 6/6/48,
>   Marion, Ohio
> Marital status: Married, 2 children
> Health: Excellent

In some cases, you may want to offer more, depending upon the nature of the job. If the job you are applying for involves physical strength, you should certainly include height and weight. The employer will want to know that you are physically capable of doing the work. That information should also be included if your physical appearance is important to the work. For example, an employer would not want to hire a salesman who is overweight.

If you are an actor, model, receptionist, hostess, airline steward or stewardess—involved in any line of work where attractiveness is important—you should include not only height and weight, but such information as color of hair and eyes as well. In some of these occupations an employer will require a photograph to accompany your résumé or application. For a fashion model, the personal data section of the résumé is most important. The employer has to know such details as physical measurements, dress, shoe, glove, and hat sizes.

If you are a foreign citizen, you should include under personal data that you have a work permit. If you are a naturalized citizen, you may either state that next to the date and place of birth, or simply leave it out. Of course, for some jobs, it might be to your advantage and a

benefit to your employer if you are bilingual or have a familiarity with foreign countries and cultures.

Under Equal Employment Opportunity guidelines, you are protected from discrimination because of race, sex, and age. It is unnecessary to mention your race or sex, but you should be willing to reveal your age by stating your date of birth. By withholding required information, you will indicate a defensive attitude about it.

In divulging your marital status, you should offer neither too little nor too much. Either being married or being single may work on your behalf. If you are married and have children, the employer assumes that you are a responsible person who wants a permanent job in order to give financial support and stability to your dependents. If you are single, the employer will see you as a flexible person who can work overtime, travel, or even move.

Although the rate of divorce has increased, being divorced still carries a negative connotation for most people, and employers are no exception. It doesn't matter how well you have coped with your divorce, nor how open-minded an employer is; the word still carries an association of disruption and instability. If you are divorced, it is advisable to give your marital status as "single," even if it has to be "single, two children." If an employer asks you about it, you may have to explain that you were divorced and carry the responsibility for your children. The word "single" indicates that you consider your status a positive one and you are not overly concerned about being divorced.

If you are widowed, you may state that fact. There are no negative associations for someone who has lost a husband or wife. On the contrary, you may gain sympathy and respect for your ability to continue in the face of adversity. This is particularly true for a housewife seeking employment in order to support herself and her children after the death of a husband.

In describing the state of your health, only one statement works entirely in your favor, and that is "excellent." However, "good" and "fair" will not work against you if your résumé is strong in every other respect. If you are in poor health, you must face the fact that you have an employment problem. Under no circumstances should you lie about having a serious illness or deficiency. In many lines of work, you will be required to undergo a medical examination, and your health problem will undoubtedly be uncovered. Even if it is a condition that is not apparent on a superficial examination, you may lose your job and be deprived of a good reference should that condition suddenly disrupt your work.

If you have a physical handicap, you should not be shy about indicating that on your résumé. Not stating it suggests that you are insecure and have not yet come to terms with the disability yourself. The strongest factor in favor of a handicapped worker is a positive, determined attitude. If you are objective about your handicap, your employer will be too. If you are bitter, resentful, or self-conscious about it, the employer will find some excuse not to hire you.

In a résumé that is weak on employment, skills, or education, you may wish to highlight the personal data by including character traits that show your potential as an employee. But be very careful about how you do this, and be prepared to substantiate your statements. If you claim initiative and resourcefulness, you should be able to tell an interviewer some way in which you displayed these qualities. If you listen and take instructions well, tell a story to illustrate the claim. Remember: You must be able to live up to any expectations your résumé places in the mind of an employer.

References

Today, most résumés do not include a list of references. Most job applicants merely state at the bottom of their résumés: "References supplied upon request." No matter what type of job you are applying for, you should be prepared to supply three personal and three business references who will attest to your character and your capabilities. That is the maximum generally required by employers, though many accept fewer.

Before submitting a name as a reference, however, you must be sure to obtain permis-

sion. Neither friends nor former employers will appreciate being taken by surprise by a request from out-of-the-blue. It is also important for you to be sure you will get a good reference before using a particular name. A conscientious employer should warn you before saying anything negative about your work performance.

There are specific reasons for leaving your references' names, addresses, and phone numbers off the résumé. If an interviewer asks you for that information it is a sign of genuine interest, and you may be able to prepare the reference for a phone call or letter for a specific job. Also, if you are going to be submitting résumés to a great many different employers, it is inconsiderate to expect your references to respond to many calls. Also, if you are considering several different jobs, you may wish to vary the names you use as references. And finally, there is the matter of space: The list of references might take up space on your résumé that could be better used for listing qualifications and experience.

On a résumé that shows little experience or skill, it might be helpful to list the name of at least one reference who can attest to the applicant's character, personality, and sincerity. For a beginning worker, a good reference from someone highly regarded can be an important asset. Of course, you must have permission to use the reference's name, and this reference should come from someone who can be considered objective as well as sympathetic.

5. The Appearance of Your Résumé

The look of your résumé is almost as important as its content. It is crucial that the presentation of facts be neat, orderly, and easy to read, with a good balance between the typed information and the white space around it. This may present some problems if you have a lot of information to include, but you can impress a prospective employer by the manner in which you solve these problems.

With very few exceptions, a résumé should be typed on a single sheet of 8½-by-11-inch white paper. Even if you think it is absolutely impossible to get all the essential data onto one page, you should make the effort to do so. An employer's first glance is a critical one; he will get an impression—good or bad—from a single page. If much of the information runs over to a second, third, or fourth page, it will not be included in his first impression.

If you have an extensive background, it is much more effective to present your entire career in brief on a single page, and attach pages of Supplementary Data to fill in the details. (See the example on pages 29–30.) By doing this, you will impress the employer by your ability to be brief and to the point. Do not overburden him with the details of your past accomplishments. You should not worry that some talent, skill, or experience will be missed by the prospective employer. Your skill at brevity will impress him sufficiently to make him eager to proceed to read the supplementary data thoroughly.

Remember: A résumé is a brief summary; it is not a full, detailed account of your life and experience. That falls under the definition of autobiography.

You should not attempt to make your résumé too artistic. Of course, if you are a commercial artist, you might want to use your résumé to demonstrate your talent, but even then you must realize that the principal object of a résumé is to communicate facts clearly and simply. Drawings and typographical decorations may attract attention; but they are also distractions that can give an impression of vanity, capriciousness, or even silliness.

Your typewriter has everything you need to create an attractive résumé—and more. Don't be tempted to use the dollar sign, the ampersand, the percent, # sign, or the asterisk in inappropriate ways. If you wish to create distinctive divisions, such as those used in most of the examples included here, simple lines will suffice. They can be made either with the key for underlining or the period key. However, don't carry this too far. Lines for dividing the major categories are all that are necessary. Placing lines around every separate piece of information makes the résumé appear even

more cluttered than it would with no lines at all.

Your objectives in laying out your résumé should be clarity and immediate communication. In looking at any flat surface, you should remember that your eyes are naturally drawn to the very center, unless that surface is broken up by color or pattern, then your eyes are attracted by the brightest or boldest aspect. If you grew up in the western world, your eyes were trained to read a piece of paper starting at the top left-hand corner, following the message down to the bottom right-hand corner.

You can use various means to interrupt the eye in its progress, especially if it is following a pattern created by type. The way you interrupt (or do not interrupt) the eye creates an emotional or sensory response. You can communicate instantly—or confuse totally. The interruption can make someone angry or irritable as easily as it can make that person feel comfortable or relaxed. It can make someone pause to contemplate, or it can move the eye along so quickly that nothing is conveyed at all.

Consequently, a certain résumé format has come to be accepted as standard. Placement of your name, address, and phone number at the top of the page not only gives this information prominence, but also evokes a response of anticipation or expectation. Placing it in the center of the top of the page heightens that response, and adds a sense of balance, assurance, and confidence. That response is sustained by centering the job objective directly below. If you separate the job objective with lines above and below it, the eye will stop momentarily for reflection before proceeding to the more extensive information that comes next, generally a description of your skills and experience.

That information comes at the middle of the page, the place where the eye is most comfortable. If this section is divided into two columns, the left column receives emphasis. If reliability and steadiness of employment are to be emphasized, the left column should be devoted to the dates of employment. If extensive responsibility and experience are to be emphasized, place the positions on the left. If

EXAMPLE VIII

DONALD DOE
0000 Craft Street
Midland, Arizona 00000
(333) 333-3333

JOB OBJECTIVE

Position as Civil Engineer, preferably with city or town.

WORK EXPERIENCE

Assistant City Engineer | City of Midland, Arizona (1971–present)

Structural Engineer | Smith & Jones Construction, Inc. (1970–1971), Midland, Arizona

Project Engineer | T-Construction International (1967–1970), San Diego, California

Structural Design Engineer | Hightower & Lake, Inc., (1964–1967), San Diego, California

Structural Designer | Northwest Foundry Company (1959–1964), Redwood, Washington

Structural Steel Detailer | MacKay & MacKay, Inc. (1956–1959), Tulsa, Oklahoma

---

EDUCATION

B.S. in Civil Engineering, Oklahoma Institute of Technology, 1956. Graduated with B average; member of Chi Epsilon, National Civil Engineering Honor Society.

Cherokee, Oklahoma Public Schools (1937–1949).

MILITARY

U.S. Marine Corps VMJ-3, 3rd Marine Air Wing; Sgt., Aerial Photographer; Honorable Discharge.

PERSONAL

Born: March 15, 1931, Cherokee, Oklahoma
Status: Married, three children
Height: 5′ 11″
Weight: 180 lbs.
Health: Excellent

References provided on request.

(EXAMPLE VIII cont.)

DONALD DOE
0000 Craft Street
Midland, Arizona 00000
(333) 333-3333

SUPPLEMENTARY DATA

WORK EXPERIENCE

Assistant City Engineer, City of Midland

Responsible for the management of various solid waste projects with concern for environmental safety.

Supervised incinerator rehabilitation.

Established criteria for an equipment maintenance facility and for drainage and sewer projects.

Assisted in the planning, organizing, and supervision of public works construction projects.

Structural Engineer, Smith & Jones Construction, Inc.

Arranged and supervised the design and engineering of a new multimillion dollar chemical plant for Universal Paints & Dyes.

Project Engineer, T-Construction International

Supervised construction of a series of structures requiring the testing and handling of sophisticated mechanical, optical, and electrical equipment. In addition to the standard structural requirements, these had to fulfill requirements for natural frequency, stiffness, and thermal considerations.

Structural Design Engineer, Hightower & Lake, Inc.

Served as designer, checker, and squad leader in the construction of various processing plants. Had specific responsibility for the structural requirements of steel and concrete for multistory buildings, a water-treatment building, storage buildings, and conveyor towers.

Structural Designer, Northwest Foundry Company

Designed, detailed, and checked components of ground support equipment for various missile programs, such as Titan, Atlas, Minuteman, Gemini, and various simulators.

Structural Steel Detailer, MacKay & MacKay, Inc.

Detailed and checked all types of heavy steel structures, including bridges, multistory office buildings, power plants, theaters, grandstands, apartment houses, and schools.

different skills applied to different jobs, they may be set off in the left column. Added emphasis can be given by underlining or typing entirely in capital letters. (However, do not overuse capital letters or underlining. Too much emphasis creates confusion.)

Generally it is not advisable to separate the two columns with a vertical line. This minimizes the importance of the information in the right column, and draws the eye down the left column directly into the information below. If education, military record, or personal data are far more important on your résumé than skills or experience, by all means use this technique.

The less the reader's eye is stopped while reviewing the résumé, the better the response. If you have created an effect of expectation and promise, you don't want to dull that. If possible, avoid a double column altogether, and keep your wording brief and simple.

If you can't type, or if you want assistance in laying out your résumé, take it to a typist. Some large cities have print-shops that specialize in printing or duplicating résumés, and they will be willing to help you for a fee. For most jobs, however, it is not necessary to go to a high-priced job consultant, who will write your résumé for you. Your own ability to create a résumé will be much more important to an employer.

When you have completed your résumé, you will want to make copies. Xerox or dry-copying is the least expensive and most satisfactory. However, do not confuse the wet process of photocopying for the dry. The slick, often muddy, quality of the copies will defeat all your good efforts; it is neither pleasant to the eye nor pleasant to the touch.

Also, ask for a sample copy before deciding on the copier. If the machines at the copy service are not functioning properly, you will get poor quality copies. A good service should be able to give you copies that are almost indistinguishable from the original.

Multilith (or offset) copies are also a possibility, but generally these are offered in quantities of a hundred. It is doubtful if you will need that many copies, even if you are planning a broadcast blind submission.

You may type each copy of your résumé individually, but this could be a wearisome task if you need a great many copies. Most employers will be impressed by receiving a typed original, but no employer expects it. If you intend to submit only two or three résumés, you might choose this alternative, but be sure you remember to keep a copy for yourself. Once you have given out a résumé, do not ask for it back. It's not only embarrassing, but may seem offensive.

Remember: The résumé is your representative. Its content, appearance, and use should always reflect the very best about you.

Part II
Finding the Right Job

6. Making the Résumé Work for You

You have created a clear, concise, positive résumé that highlights the best features of your background, experience, and objectives.

Now all you need is the job opening.

Admittedly, finding the right job is not always an easy task, especially if you are a young person entering the job market for the first time or a woman going back to work after a long absence. The first obstacle to overcome is your own fear and apprehension about how employers will respond to you. It's natural to have a bit of stage fright or a few butterflies in your stomach before setting out to find a job; everyone feels that way. However, you must not allow yourself to procrastinate after you have completed the résumé. Allow the surge of self-confidence you feel and the positive incentive you gained to work for you.

In finding a job, you have a variety of methods to choose from. In each of them, your résumé can play a major role.

The first important work your résumé can do is to help you break through the barrier of your own hesitation. With an actor, stage fright disappears as soon as he is on stage with something tangible to do—an action to perform, a line of dialogue to speak, a character or a prop to relate to. Your résumé is something tangible for you to rely on in a similar manner. It is your introduction to the employer or personnel director. Whether you mail it, deliver it by hand, or send it through a personnel agency, it will place you on a personal basis with an employer.

7. The Blind Approach: Writing a Cover Letter

In most large businesses, employers are accustomed to receiving résumés mailed to them blindly. They usually will respond only if they happen to have the precise job opening you seek at that particular time. Some employers keep résumés on file for a month or two, but then they consider that you have found the position you seek.

If you follow the blind or scattershot approach in mailing out résumés, you are depending a great deal on chance, and you must be prepared for a negative reply or even no answer at all. Most important, you must not allow negative responses to demoralize you. If you do not get an interview, you should not take it personally. An employer who does not have a position open will not want to waste your time or his.

In many cases, however, the blind approach can be one of the best means of finding and getting a job. If you are lucky, your résumé could land on the employer's desk at precisely the right moment and catch his attention even before he has begun the search for someone to fill a position. Or, if your résumé is particularly noteworthy, he may keep it on file for some time just in case a need arises in the future.

For best results, the blind approach should not be entirely blind. The more you know about the companies to which you mail your résumés, the greater will be your advantage. At the very least, you should have the names of the department heads or personnel directors.

A letter addressed "to whom it may concern" may not reach anyone, and you will have wasted a stamp and a résumé.

Approach the process step by step:

a) Obtain the names and addresses of all companies that might hire you. If you have a clearly defined job objective, this should not be difficult to do. You may even have such a list. If not, find out if there is a trade journal or publication for the specific business or industry. Or, simply use the Yellow Pages of your phone book. Your local library may be able to help you, especially if the businesses or industries are in cities other than where you presently live. If you are in college, your dean or guidance counselor should be able to assist you.

b) Narrow the list if necessary. In most situations, there will be more companies than you can possibly hope to send résumés to, so limit yourself to the ten or twelve best ones for your purposes. Consider the location, the size, and the reputation of the specific companies to narrow your list.

c) Find the name and title of the person who does the hiring for your job. This may be a personnel director, a foreman, a department head, or a company owner or official. If you have no other resource for this information, telephone the companies and obtain the necessary names from the switchboard or receptionist.

d) Write your covering letter and mail it with your résumé. The letter should be brief, straightforward, and succinct, stating little more than your desire to be considered for a job when an opening should arise. Your résumé conveys everything else. (See Example IX on page 33 for a sample letter.) This brief letter gets your point across and shows your consideration in not taking up a great deal of

EXAMPLE IX
The Blind Letter
_____

1234 Willow Lane
Lake Milton, Alabama 00000
September 5, 1980

Mr. Albert Jones
Vice-President
The Holt-Wilburn Company
12345 West Plains Street
Nyack, New York 11111

Dear Mr. Jones:

Your company has been recommended to me as one of the finest in the field of paper and cardboard containers. I am told that you are expanding and are seeking young and talented designers.

I am enclosing my résumé in the hope that you might have a position for which I am qualified. If there is no opening at the present time, perhaps you could keep my résumé on file for consideration at a later date.

Thank you for your attention.

Sincerely,

Gerald Smith

the recipient's time. Each letter you send should be typed individually. While your résumé may be a photocopy, your covering letter should not. No employer will respond to a letter mailed out in circular fashion. It tells him that you are sending copies indiscriminately to the industry, and insults him by implying that his company is no different from the rest. An individual letter distinguishes him and his company. By taking the time and trouble to single him out, you increase the likelihood that he will take the time and trouble to reply.

8. Answering Want Ads

For most people, job hunting is limited to the classified ads in the local newspaper. It may be your solution as well. Certainly, it is the most direct way of finding out what jobs are available in your city; the fact that an employer has advertised his need for an employee does take much of the apprehension out of the job search. Most ads list the job title, the minimum qualifications required, the name of the company, and how to respond.

For example:

Receptionist

BEGINNER

Growing co. has immediate opening for receptionist with good voice & typing skills. Will train. Call 123-4567 for appt.

This is a straightforward ad, with an emphasis on having a good telephone voice. A phone call is all that is required to get the interview. (This is in fact a part of the interview.) Another ad might give the name of the company and ask the applicant to apply in person to the personnel director.

Some ads, however, conceal the name of the company and its location. This is done for one of two reasons: Either the company wants to avoid large numbers of applicants showing up at its doors, or the company wants to hire someone new before letting the present em-ployee go. The applicant is asked to send a résumé with a covering letter to a newspaper box or a post office box, and he may or may not receive a reply.

Here is an example of such an ad:

CREDIT ANALYST

Major apparel company seeking experienced credit person with factoring or manufacturing background. Starting salary commensurate with experience. Excellent benefits and opportunity. Reply in confidence to:

The Jonesboro Times
Box No. T-11
1234 Main Street
Jonesboro, N.Y. 11111

The most unnerving thing about these ads is that the applicant has no idea what company he is dealing with. There have been cases in which an applicant—completely unaware that he was about to be fired—has sent a résumé and letter applying for his own job, with rather embarrassing results.

Before you respond to such an ad you should be aware of what it suggests about the nature of the company and how it treats its employees. These ads are not usually placed by companies that treat employees with respect as individuals, but rather indicate companies that wish to maintain an advantage over employees. If you have no difficulty subjugating yourself to an employer's rigid rules and regulations you will have no problem answering such an ad.

Much more promising, however, is an ad such as the following:

ELECTRONIC TECHNICIANS

We have immediate openings for electronic technicians with good working knowledge of basic electronics. 2 years experience necessary. Some training offered. Send résumé to:

Tom Smith
SMITH & SMITH ELECTRONICS
1234 34th Street
Traylor, Texas 77777

This ad holds nothing back; it gives the applicant the advantage of knowing all the essential information, and suggests that the employer intends to be fair. There is no hint that your job search is some sort of top secret mission that you need to be paranoid about. In sending your résumé to Tom Smith, you know it will receive personal attention and that you may receive a call or a letter in reply.

Of course, you should include a covering letter with your résumé, but it should be a letter that is short and to the point. Tell where you saw the ad and use your résumé to show that you are the person the company is looking for. If you wish, you may clip the ad from the newspaper and attach it to your letter and résumé. (See Example X on page 35 for a sample of a covering letter in response to an ad.)

9. The Personnel Approach

Some classified ads in the newspaper refer you to a personnel agency that may or may not offer legitimate prospects for you. In some states, these agencies are regulated by law and must provide the services they advertise. Under no circumstances are they allowed to charge more than the law allows. You will be required to sign a contract, agreeing to pay a

EXAMPLE X

In Answer to an Ad

2222 Overpass Street
Houston, Texas 77777
September 5, 1980

Mr. Tom Smith
Smith & Smith Electronics
1234 34th Street
Traylor, Texas 77777

Dear Mr. Smith:

In response to your ad in the Traylor *Times*, I am enclosing my résumé.

I believe I am just the person you are looking for. I am looking for a job as an Electronic Technician, and I have had almost exactly two years experience.

I am willing to learn, and eager to work.

If you wish to arrange an interview, you may reach me by phone any afternoon after two o'clock.

Thank you for your consideration.

Sincerely,

Robert Paul Doe

fee if and when the agency finds you a job, usually an amount that is minimal considering the service it provides. Some agencies have job listings with the fees paid by the employers. Their service costs you nothing. Under no circumstances, however, should you sign with an agency that requires a fee before they do their work.

Personnel agencies actually provide services for employers as well as job-seekers; in large cities, most of them specialize in particular fields or occupations. Agencies may have exclusive listings with certain companies, or get leads on whatever jobs they have available well ahead of other sources. One agency may specialize in secretaries or clerical workers, another in advertising executives or publishing executives, and yet another in computer programmers and data analysts. By looking over the ads in the newspapers, you can usually determine which ones handle your specific field. There will probably be no more than two or three.

Some personnel agencies are excellent; others may be weak and ineffectual. The best agencies will take a personal interest in you and will show enthusiasm after reading your résumé. They will be direct and honest, and will send you to interview only for the kind of jobs they feel are right for you.

There have been cases where personnel agents have taken an interest in the careers of particular applicants. Such agents establish a relationship that lasts over many years as they gradually help the applicant up the ladder, but these are rare cases. You do not have to rely on a single agency to work for you; you may register with as many agencies as there are in your field. However, if two agents refer you to the same job, you should advise the second one that you have already applied for it so that there is no confusion over who gets paid the fee.

Treat the employment agent with as much respect as you would an employer. His or her attitude toward you is extremely important. Always be on time for appointments, and call or report back to the agent on interviews or subsequent calls from a prospective employer. If there is interest from an employer the em-

ployment agent will be pushing for you. He or she could be the factor that finally convinces the employer to hire you.

Always notify the agency when you have accepted a position, whether or not that agency has gotten you the job. You needn't feel shy about saying another agent is responsible; the important thing is that you keep the agents' respect by not having them work for you longer than necessary.

10. The Personal Approach

One of the most successful ways of getting jobs is also one of the least talked about. Applicants who come highly recommended through respected employees often get preferential treatment. A résumé that comes to an employer through someone he knows and trusts will certainly be looked at before one that comes impersonally through the mail.

If you know someone who works where you want to work you have a head start. If that person has a high regard for you, you should have no reservation at all about asking the favor.

Once you have been in an industry for a while, you may know employees in a number of other companies. Even if you feel squeamish about using your friendships to get jobs, you will certainly want to maintain contact so that you will hear when jobs become available. The day is long past when an employee begins at the bottom rung of the ladder at one company and remains with that company until retirement. The way to move up in business today, to receive promotions and pay increases in rapid succession, is to move among the companies within your field. Therefore, the industry grapevine is important to you and to your friends.

So don't overlook this possibility.

11. Advertising Yourself

Sometimes the usual channels just don't work. Your particular talents don't seem to fit into the standard job requirements, or the job you're looking for isn't available at the moment. You may find it does pay to advertise.

Most newspapers have a section of Situations Wanted ads on their classified pages. It's often one of the least filled columns in the paper. But employers do sometimes glance through the listings, and you could find exactly the job you're looking for by advertising yourself. It can be rather expensive to run the ad for any length of time, and you are taking a chance on its being seen; however, if you're a gambler, you might want to try it.

Of course, wording is most important. You must catch an employer's eye with very few words. Pick out the most salient points from your job objective and your skills or experience. Try to determine the one most outstanding feature to highlight the ad. Is it the job you seek? Or is it a particular talent?

If you are in doubt about which approach to use, try writing the ad both ways, then determine which one you think will be most likely to catch the eye.

In this ad, the talent is placed first:

GOOD AT ORGANIZING

Admin. Asst., 8 yrs. exp. Seeks challenging job w. busy exec. Type 80 wpm. Box X834 Times.

All of the most important facts are there. The woman does not mention that she has taken off twenty years to bring up two children. That will be discussed in the interview after the employer has been sufficiently impressed with her abilities.

Here is an example that places the job objective first:

MECH. ENGINEER

Recent grad., willing to relocate. Seeks opportunity to grow with small company. Box X834 Times.

You may use more words than these examples do, but only if you have more specific qualifications to offer. Don't waste money on unnecessary frills. The objective is to gain an employer's attention, and too many words reduce the chance of your ad's being read in its entirety.

You should respond to all the inquiries you receive, whether or not you send your résumé or arrange for an interview. Every employer who has taken the time and trouble to answer your ad deserves a personal reply, even if it merely thanks him for his letter and gives a reason for not accepting an interview. Although your ad may be anonymous and your failure to respond will not harm your career in any way, you do decrease that employer's willingness to use the situations wanted columns again.

If your ad succeeds, you might want to use the same approach the next time you're looking for a job.

Part III
Getting the Right Job

12. Steps and Sidesteps

Your résumé is a promise that you must be able to fulfill. If you can maintain the positive and objective problem-solving attitude you used in creating the résumé, you should have little difficulty in getting and holding the position you want. Keep your job objective in sight and maintain confidence in your abilities.

Whether you are applying for your first job or one of a succession of jobs, remember that each job should help you achieve your career goal. A job objective is not always synonymous with a career goal, but it should be related. A paycheck should be only a part of what you get from a job well done. You should be learning, growing, and acquiring skills and respect that will serve you well in the next stage of your career.

Perhaps too much emphasis is placed on "being happy" in your work. It's rare that work makes one happy. Much more important is a sense of satisfaction with yourself and the job you are doing, a pride in accomplishment, and a realization that you are working toward a goal. If you are building your career carefully, step by step, that is what you should experience.

If you are unhappy in your job—which means you do not have that sense of satisfaction—perhaps you are in the wrong line of work. There is no disgrace in changing careers at any stage of life. Don't flounder in a line of work you do not enjoy. The enthusiasm you feel when facing the challenge of finding a new line of work can make up for almost any lack in your background.

Most employers expect employees to take predictable steps up the ladder of success, and admittedly they think it odd when someone breaks that pattern. However, there are ways of taking sidesteps in your career that will only command respect.

If you have what might be considered an employment problem—if you are a housewife going back to work after a long absence, a worker changing careers, or someone for whom long unemployment has made a change necessary—you can show your sincerity and enthusiasm by sidestepping. Going back to school is perhaps the best example of this procedure. A housewife may register for night classes as tangible proof that she is sincere in her desire to hold a regular job. A high-school dropout may go for his GED (high school equivalency diploma) as an indication that he has resolved his problems, or a college dropout may go back to complete his degree.

As long as you can substantiate your goals, an employer will take your enthusiasm seriously. It is as important to him as it is to you that you get the right job. Your sense of satisfaction in your job means that you are doing his work well.

13. Attitude, Manner, and Appearance

The job interview is a critical stage of the job-getting process. If an employer has received your résumé by mail or through an employment agent, he will have formed an impression of you as clear-headed, capable, and bright. Don't hurt your chances at this stage by carelessness in your manner and appearance. Live up to his expectations.

This is not to suggest that every man should wear a hat, a suit, and a tie, or that every woman should wear a dress, high heels, and a pair of white gloves, or that either should behave as if attending a tea party.

Your attitude, manner, and appearance should match the job you are seeking. Your employer will not want a misfit. If you have any doubt about what is customary for the job level, or the company, find out before you go for the interview.

As a general rule, you would not go to an interview for an office job wearing old blue jeans, nor would you apply for a job as a manual laborer wearing a suit and tie. Most office jobs still require a man to wear a tie, with a suit or sport jacket; and, although many offices now accept women in attractive pants outfits, it is generally advisable for a woman to appear at an interview wearing a dress, suit, or skirt and blouse. If the company has more relaxed dress rules, you can adjust to them later.

In almost all occupations, however, neatness and cleanliness count. In an employer's mind, they are always indicative of a conscientious, careful person, who respects himself as well as others. Hair well-kept and of a reasonable length, fingernails clean and trimmed, clothing that is attractive and comfortable, and shoes that are neat and functional all contribute toward a good impression.

Use your judgment on details. For example, a typist would not have excessively long or highly painted nails; an executive who entertains at business lunches would dress stylishly; a receptionist would give special attention to hair and makeup.

Your attitude and your manner are just as important as your physical appearance. Although employers make some allowance for an applicant's natural nervousness in job interviews, your ability to control your feelings is important. If possible, you should be relaxed, but alert and attentive. You should be friendly and direct without getting too personal. Show an interest in whatever the interviewer has to say, and your willingness to be cooperative in any way you can.

Moodiness, sullenness, anxiety, arrogance, boisterous laughter—all have no place in the business world, and so should not be exhibited in an interview.

Unless otherwise instructed, you should address the interviewer as Mr., Miss, or Mrs. When asked to sit, do not slouch or lounge. Don't smoke unless the interviewer suggests that you may. Be patient about getting in your own questions or comments. Let the interviewer lead the interview. When he is done, you will have ample opportunity to ask questions.

14. Rehearsal

If you are not experienced at interviews and have doubts about how to present yourself, you may wish to prepare yourself with a "rehearsal." While there is no way you can prepare yourself fully for what will take place, a rehearsal for the interview gives you a good opportunity to consider the possibilities and helps you feel more confident and assured.

You may ask a friend or family member to rehearse with you, or you may do it alone. Your object is to catch yourself in any mistakes you might make, and eliminate as many of them as possible. If you have difficulty accepting criticism from others, by all means do your rehearsing by yourself. You do not want rehearsal to increase your nervousness.

If possible, dress as you intend to for the interview. Study yourself in the mirror to determine if you are presenting yourself in the best possible way. Try to be objective. Do you look like a person who is efficient, hard-working, neat, careful, energetic, and pleasant? Check yourself from head to toe—your hair, your suit or dress, your hands, your shoes. Would you trust a man or woman who dressed this way? Do what you can to correct any faults you find.

Next, consider the person who is interviewing you. Can you remember his or her name? If you can't, check your appointment notes. Memorize the name and speak it aloud several times so that it comes easily to your lips. Make sure you preface the name with Mr., Miss, or Mrs.

Practice entering the room and greeting the interviewer. Check your posture. The interviewer will probably offer his or her hand to shake. Be prepared for a brief, friendly, firm handshake, but don't make it too firm. You should also be prepared not to shake hands. The interviewer may simply rise from behind a desk and ask you to sit down.

Rehearse how you sit. Using both an upholstered chair and a simple straight-backed chair. In each, determine the position in which you feel most comfortable yet capable of appearing alert and interested. Try two different approaches. Lean back in the chair. Do you seem too relaxed, too comfortable? Do you appear to be lounging? If so, try sitting forward on the edge of the chair with your back straight and your legs crossed at the ankles. If you are not uncomfortable in this position, it may be the better one for you. In most cases, it gives the impression that you are alert and eager.

Take two copies of your résumé with you. You will want to have a copy so that you can refer to it yourself. The second copy is a spare, just in case the interviewer has not received one, or if he has misplaced the one he received. Determine how you will carry these résumés with you. They should never be folded and stuffed into a pocket or purse. If you do not carry a briefcase, keep the résumés discreetly concealed yet neat in a plain 9-x 12-inch manila envelope. You may also carry with you almost any material that can substantiate your résumé. (Some applicants may have samples of work, letters of commendation, lists of references or business contacts, or expanded substantiating résumés.)

Study your résumé and try to guess what sort of questions the interviewer may ask. (If you need help, refer to the various sample résumés, but relate them to your own.) Consider what questions you have about the job—hours, pay, working conditions, benefits, and so on. Remind yourself to be patient about asking these questions. It's not wise to appear too eager to obtain this information. Don't attempt to take over the interview; let the interviewer lead you.

Practice leaving the interview. The interviewer will generally let you know when it is over, either by saying so or by rising and saying, "Thank you for coming." Don't try to prolong the interview past this point. Do be sure to thank the interviewer for his or her time; and, if the interviewer has not offered the information, you may ask when the company expects to have made a decision. But do not try to hold the interviewer in conversation.

15. The Interview

Try to arrive for your interview precisely at the time appointed. Do not be late. You may arrive a few minutes early, but do not arrive more than ten minutes before the appointed time. You don't want to appear too anxious, and it may annoy the interviewer to know that you are waiting.

Interviewers come in all shapes, sizes, and degrees of ability, from the shrewd and cunning, to the honest and straightforward, to the incompetent. You must be prepared for almost anything so that you will not be taken by surprise and do or say something inappropriate. Whatever manner an interviewer assumes, accept it, and do your best to behave naturally.

Remember: The interviewer is human too.

Anything that appears on your résumé is fair game for questions from the interviewer. Some will look for information they can relate to themselves—a place you have lived or worked or gone to school—and will use it to start the interview on a familiar or friendly level. Others will begin with a description of the job opening and the qualifications needed for it.

Some will ask questions that are clearly answered on your résumé. Don't be surprised at this, and don't refer the interviewer to the résumé for the answer. If the interviewer has not read your résumé carefully, you don't want to offend him by pointing out his oversight. It is possible he has read it and is simply looking for a way of drawing you into conversation so he can judge the way you speak and handle yourself.

Most questions will fall into the following categories:

a) Your job objective and career goals. The interviewer will want to find out how dedicated and determined you are to achieve success and how clearly you express your objectives. He will assess whether you consider the job a temporary step on your ladder or if you are making a permanent commitment. It is very important how you answer these questions. No matter how friendly the interviewer is, no matter how interested he seems in your welfare, remember that his first concern is his company.

Examples of such questions are:

(1) Why do you want this job?
(2) Why do you want to work for our company?
(3) What are your long-term career goals?
(4) Do you feel this job would be a long-term commitment?
(5) Are you willing to work overtime?
(6) What do you think this job can teach you?

b) Your skills, experience, and work record. This can be the most critical part of the interview, though not always the decisive part. By knowing your past work record, the interviewer will try to learn what talents and abilities you have, and how you will fit into his organization. He will look for your strengths and weaknesses, and he will compare you with the other applicants. Be careful how you answer these questions. If there are any negative facts in your past record, be truthful, but do not dwell on them; state the case as objectively and as unemotionally as possible. If you were fired, you will have to say so; if you did not get along with a former boss or with co-workers, tell the truth, but don't harp on the faults of others.

Examples of questions that might be asked are:

(1) Why did you leave your last job?
(2) Do you feel you can handle this job?
(3) What special skills can you contribute toward this job?
(4) Do you know how to perform all the tasks necessary?
(5) Have you ever been fired from a job?
(6) Do you generally get along with your co-workers?
(7) Do you take orders (or instructions) easily?
(8) What do you do when you are faced with a problem you can't handle?
(9) Are you willing to travel?
(10) How long were you employed at your last job?
(11) What do you feel is your greatest weakness?
(12) What is your greatest strength?
(13) Have you ever been unemployed for any length of time?
(14) Are you punctual for work and appointments?

c) Your educational background. If you have had considerable work experience, the interviewer may not dwell very long on your education; but if you are applying for your first job, or one in a new line of work, this will be an important part of the interview. The questions should be directed toward your ability to do the job but, if they are not, your answers should attempt to relate your capabilities without being too obtrusive.

Some questions that might be asked are:

(1) Did you graduate from college (or high school)?
(2) What was your standing in your class? What sort of grade average did you have?

(3) Did you like school?

(4) How did you get along with your teachers?

(5) Did you have a good attendance record?

(6) How did you finance your college education?

(7) Did you participate in extracurricular activities?

(8) Did you receive any honors?

(9) Did you change your course of study? If so, why?

(10) What were your strongest and weakest subjects in school?

(11) Are you taking any courses now? Do you intend to go back to school for any further courses?

d) Your personal life. An employer is entitled to know some personal information about you. You should not hesitate to answer. But the personal questions should be restricted to the most basic facts. In jobs where an employee deals with money or has access to confidential information, however, the employer is entitled to know more. There are laws governing what information employers are entitled to know. If there are sensitive areas of your personal life or background, you may wish to check these laws to determine how you should answer. (For example, an employer may ask if you have ever been convicted of a crime. However, he cannot ask if you have ever been arrested.)

Personal question you should be prepared to answer are:

(1) How old are you?

(2) Are you married or single?

(3) Do you have any children?

(4) Do you own your own home, or do you rent?

(5) How is your health?

(6) Do you have any health problems that affect the job?

(7) What are your hobbies?

(8) How do you generally spend your spare time?

(9) Do you play any sports?

(10) Do you belong to any professional organizations?

(11) Do you have any relatives in the same line of work?

(12) Are your parents living?

(13) How many brothers and sisters do you have?

Questions about religion and politics are out of place in a job interview. If an interviewer should ask about either of these, try to answer in a way that is not offensive. By asking such a question, the interviewer indicates that it is important to him, so a noncommittal answer can be as bad as the wrong answer. You will have to use your own judgment for a careful response.

e) Your salary and financial obligations. Again, this can be a sensitive area, but you should be willing to answer most questions regarding money directly and honestly. Your financial obligations are of concern only in occupations that involve sensitive financial transactions. Such questions are asked only to determine your honesty and reliability. If you have something to hide, you are probably in the wrong line of work.

Questions that may be asked are:

(1) What salary do you expect (or require)?

(2) What was your salary at your last job?

(3) Do you manage to live adequately on that amount?

(4) Do you have any outstanding debts?

(5) Is your home paid for?

(6) Have you ever been bonded?

(7) Do you have dependents other than your immediate family?

There are certain questions you should be prepared to ask if the interviewer does not offer the information. However, try to save your questions until it is quite obvious the interview is finished. A good interviewer will ask you at the appropriate time if you have any questions.

Some things you might want to know are:

(1) What is the salary for this job?

(2) How is the salary paid—weekly, bimonthly, monthly?

(3) What benefits does the company offer?

(4) What are the working hours?

(5) Is there pay for overtime?

(6) How often does the company review for raises?

(7) Does the company generally promote from within?

(8) Is there traveling involved in the job?

(9) Is there entertainment involved, and if so, are such expenses paid by the company?

(10) When does the job start?

(11) When does the company expect to make a decision?

You should leave the interview on an optimistic, enthusiastic note. Express your pleasure at meeting the interviewer, and thank the person for his or her time.

16. The Follow-up

You may be offered the job at the interview. If you are, it's the exception, rather than the rule. Usually there is a lapse of time between the interview and the decision to hire, and often your part in that decision is not over. You may be asked to return for further interviews. (The more important the job, the greater the number of people involved in the decision to hire.) Often an employer has agreed to meet a number of applicants, and wants to give himself the opportunity to consider each fairly.

At the close of your interview, get some idea of when you will next have contact with the employer. The interviewer should tell you whether you will hear if you have the job or not, and when you can expect to know. He may ask you to call on a certain date or he may want to call you. Or, the information can be communicated by an employment agency.

Unless he has specifically asked you to call his office, an employer will feel pressured if you call to find out about his decision. It is difficult to be patient, but you should make the effort.

One of the advantages of using an employment agency is that you will usually be told the results of your interview as soon as they are known. If you did not get the job, the agency will tell you why and may offer helpful suggestions on how to avoid the problem at your next interview.

17. After You Get the Job

Once you have the job, you must be able to keep it. Employees always expect employers to live up to any promises made in the interview, but often they forget about their own promises.

Keep your enthusiasm going. Be on time for work. Take orders and instruction cheerfully. Realize you are moving into a work situation that was established long before you arrived. Not only will your new boss be watching you, but also your fellow workers. It is wise to prepare for the actual working environment. The employees may be looking forward to your arrival with happy expectancy, or awaiting you with suspicion or jealousy. You will have to prove yourself to them as well as to your employer.

You may naturally feel apprehensive about fitting into the job environment, but you should not allow your anxiety to disrupt your work. Don't boast or compare your new job unfavorably with your last.

First impressions are always important because they are often lasting impressions.

Part IV
Sample Résumés

18. Dealing with Your Résumé Problems

Because it is unlikely that your résumé problems are identical to anyone else's, no single résumé in this book can possibly deal with the precise mixture of problems you face in your chosen occupation. However, by studying a variety of résumés, you can see how others have dealt with their own special needs. Most major problems are covered in one résumé or another, though the example may not be in your job field.

No attempt has been made to give résumés for every occupation; there are far too many different kinds of jobs for any single book to cover them all. In such a book, you could hope to find only one page that is relevant for you, and the remainder of the pages would be a waste of your money. In those existing books that do cover a wide range of jobs, the sample résumés are invariably at a high level of experience, and they are totally useless to someone who is just setting out into the job market.

The sample résumés that follow show a broad range of occupations, but these résumés emphasize the levels of employment rather than the specific job title. Each résumé is based on a real case, though all have been altered to protect anonymity. If you are just beginning the job search, those résumés for inexperienced workers will be most helpful to you because they deal with similar problems. If you have been working for some time, you can pick out the résumés that reflect your own level of experience to see how others have conveyed their background.

And, if you have serious résumé problems, such as a change of occupation, periods of unemployment, or interrupted education, these examples show how others have successfully overcome similar handicaps.

Spend some time studying the sample résumés. You will be able to see how different résumé problems were handled by the applicants. This is an important lesson you must learn: Don't let the problems show on your résumé.

Before reading the commentaries on each case, glance at the résumé examples. See how impressive they look before you read the true stories of the applicants' careers.

EXAMPLE A

DIANNE DOE
1234 West Beach Road
Palm Bayou, Louisiana 00000
(000) 000-0000

JOB OBJECTIVE

Position as Sales Clerk with Department Store.

QUALITIES

Willing to work hard * Free evenings or days * Congenial *

Good at selling merchandise * Capable of learning

WORK EXPERIENCE

Commission Salesperson
On part-time basis, sold the Universal American Encyclopedia, 1970–1974. Attended training program sponsored by company, 1970; attended subsequent conferences of salespersons for refresher courses. Won Gold Medal Award as best salesperson for year 1973, having sold more sets of encyclopedias than anyone else in the country.
    Procedures involved calling people on the phone, telling about the Universal American Encyclopedia, and arranging for personal demonstrations in homes.

Delivery Person
The Palm Bayou *Herald,* 1972–1973. On part-time basis, delivered newspaper to local newsstands.

Commission Salesperson
Avon Products, 1968–1971. On a part-time basis, sold beauty products door-to-door.

Sales Clerk
Farley's Department Store, New Orleans, 1942–1947. Helped customers in Women's Ready-to-Wear department.

EDUCATION

Graduated from Lewis High School, New Orleans, 1943.

PERSONAL

Born: September 24, 1925; New Orleans, Louisiana.
Status: Widowed; three grown children.
Health: Excellent.

EXAMPLE B

DIANNE DOE
1234 West Beach Road
Palm Bayou, Louisiana 00000
(000) 000-0000

JOB OBJECTIVE

Position in Retail Sales or Management.

WORK EXPERIENCE

Manager, Catalog Dept.	I. J. Nichols Department Store, 1976–Present. Manage staff of five salespersons; responsible for placing computer orders; keep catalog department records; handle sales and returns.
Clerk,	I. J. Nichols Department Store, 1974–1976. Waited on customers, took orders, and occasionally placed orders on computer.
Commission Salesperson	On part-time basis, sold the Universal American encyclopedia, 1970–1974. Won Gold Medal Award as best salesperson for year 1973.
Delivery Person	The Palm Bayou *Herald*, 1972–1973. On part-time basis, delivered newspaper to local newsstands.
Commission Salesperson	Avon Products, 1968–1971. On a part-time basis, sold beauty products door-to-door.
Sales Clerk	Farley's Department Store, New Orleans, 1942–1947. Helped customers in Women's Ready-to-Wear department.

EDUCATION

Graduated from Lewis High School, New Orleans, 1943.

PERSONAL

Born: September 24, 1925; New Orleans, Louisiana.
Status: Widowed; three grown children.
Health: Excellent.

References supplied upon request.

EXAMPLE C

HELEN MARIE SMITH
000 West Oak Street
Little Falls, New Hampshire 00000
(000) 000-0000

JOB OBJECTIVE

Sales position with book publisher.

POTENTIAL

Familiar with both trade and college book sales.

Understand inventory and returns policies.

Have been responsible for placing orders and reorders.

WORK EXPERIENCE

Assistant
Bookstore Mgr.
1970–1972

- Right-hand person to the owner-manager of THE BOOK NOOK in Little Falls, New Hampshire. Assisted in maintaining stock, placing reorders, and selling.

Bookstore Clerk
(1966–1970)

- During college career, worked part-time as a salesperson at THE BOOK NOOK in Little Falls, New Hampshire.

EDUCATION

B.A., Merriwether College, Little Falls, N.H.; double major in English and History; 3.5 grade average, 1966–1970.

Diploma, Little Falls High School, Little Falls, N.H.; class valedictorian, 1966. Attended Little Falls Public Schools, 1954–1966.

HOBBIES AND ACTIVITIES

Play tennis and softball.

Write poetry.

PERSONAL

Born: June 6, 1948; Little Falls, New Hampshire
Status: Single
Health: Excellent

EXAMPLE D

HELEN MARIE SMITH
2222 North 22nd Ave.
Maiden Lane, Maine 0000
(222) 222-2222

JOB OBJECTIVE

Position as sales person with trade book publisher.

WORK EXPERIENCE

<u>Trade Book
Salesperson,</u>
1975–1980

- Sales representative, New England area, promoting line of adult and children's books for THE PETER PIPER PRESS.

<u>Textbook
Salesperson,</u>
1972–1975

- Called on college bookstores and on department chairmen in History and the Social Sciences, New England area. Representative for COLLEGE TEXT PRESS.

<u>Assistant
Bookstore Mgr.</u>
1970–1972

- Right-hand person to the owner-manager of THE BOOK NOOK in Little Falls, New Hampshire. Assisted in maintaining stock, placing reorders, and selling.

<u>Bookstore Clerk</u>
1966–1970
(part-time)

- During college career, worked part-time as salesperson at THE BOOK NOOK in Little Falls, New Hampshire.

EDUCATION

B.A., Merriwether College, Little Falls, N.H.; double major in English and History; 3.5 grade average, 1966–1970.

Diploma, Little Falls High School, Little Falls, N.H.; class valedictorian, 1966. Attended Little Falls Public Schools, 1954–1966.

HOBBIES AND ACTIVITIES

Play tennis and softball.

Write poetry; three poems published in *Yankee Review*.

PERSONAL

Born: June 6, 1948; Little Falls, New Hampshire
Height: 5′ 8″
Weight: 110 lbs.
Status: Single
Health: Excellent

19. Examples and Explanations

Examples A & B—Dianne Doe

Dianne Doe had only a high school education. She held only one job before her marriage—that of a sales clerk during World War II. After the war, she was married and lived happily as a wife and mother for twenty years before her husband became seriously and terminally ill. At the time, two of her children were in college and one was in high school. With her husband now unable to work, and with heavy medical bills, the family savings were being depleted rapidly.

She was faced with two problems: She felt she had no real qualifications for work, and there were times when her husband's health needed her attention and care. She spent a short time feeling sorry for herself, and then took the only kind of work she felt able to—selling Avon products to the people in her town. It was hardly enough to support the family, but it did help to slow the depletion of family savings.

Dianne discovered that she was good at selling. When she saw an ad for selling encyclopedias, she responded, and she was so successful that she stopped selling the Avon products after a year.

By 1973, her husband was permanently hospitalized, and she again took on a second job—delivering newspapers. Her work helped to cushion the blow when her husband died. Her two older children were grown and on their own; her third son was in college. For the year after her husband's death, she was able to support herself on what she made selling encyclopedias.

But it did not occupy her full time. At the age of 49, she decided to embark on a career. She prepared a résumé (Example A, p. 45), and set out to get a job with a department store.

She began as a sales clerk and within two years had become the head of a department. Within six years, her résumé was quite impressive. (Example B., p. 46)

Examples C & D—Helen Marie Smith

Helen Marie Smith also began as a sales clerk, but she drifted into her career less dramatically than did Dianne Doe. She started working in a bookstore while a student in college. Actually, she had no intention of having a career. Her great love was writing poetry, and she assumed she would meet a boy in college, get married, have a family, and do her writing in her spare time.

During college, however, she began to think more independently. She liked selling books, and she found that she was good at it. After graduating from college, the owner of the bookstore hired her to be assistant manager.

Within two years, she had decided on a career for herself. She wanted to travel as a sales representative for a book publisher, and hoped to eventually move into a managerial position. In 1972, however, almost all publishing salespersons were men; it was difficult for women to break into a field that required extensive traveling alone, often driving long distances at night.

But Helen Marie Smith was determined. The women's liberation movement was growing strong at the time, and she had a certain moral pressure behind her. Publishing was outwardly a liberal business; a company could be pressed to hire her, if only as a token.

She wanted to sell trade books (general fiction and nonfiction) but found that college textbook companies were more open to hiring a woman. She submitted her résumé (Example C, p. 47), and took the first job that was offered.

After three years, she was able to get the kind of position she wanted, with a trade publisher. After another five years, her résumé was quite impressive. (Example D, p. 48.)

EXAMPLE E

CHRIS JONES
123 West 12th Street
Pine Valley, Nebraska 00000
(444) 444-4444

JOB OBJECTIVE

Position as Accountant.

CAPABILITIES

Good knowledge of accounting procedures.

Have studied Budget Control, Auditing, Taxation and Finance, and Public Administration.

Good bookkeeper.

WORK EXPERIENCE

1965–1968	During college, did free-lance work preparing tax returns.
Summers 1965–1968	Worked as clerk in State Tax Office.

EDUCATION

Bachelor of Business Administration, Hardee College, 1968. Graduated near the top of the class, with a 3.5 Grade Average.

Graduated from West Deerfield Public Schools, 1964. Participated in Advanced Math Program. Graduated second in class.

HOBBIES AND ACTIVITIES

Play tennis and golf.

PERSONAL

Born: July 6, 1946, West Deerfield, Nebraska
Height: 5′ 9″
Weight: 135 lbs.
Status: Single
Health: Excellent

References provided on request.

EXAMPLE F

CHRIS JONES
123 West 12th Street
Pine Valley, Nebraska 00000
(444) 444-4444

JOB OBJECTIVE

Position in City Management.

EXPERIENCE

1972–Present | Director of Finance, City of Pine Valley. Supervise the departments of Accounting, Personnel, Budget Control, Internal Auditing, Purchasing, and Treasury. Charged with seeing that all monies are received properly and all expenditures are made according to the city budget.

1970–1972 | Department Head, Budget Control, City of Pine Valley. Assisted the City Manager in preparing the budget and in controlling the administration of the budget.

1968–1970 | Accountant, Madewell & Barton, Certified Public Accountants. Involved in accounting, auditing, and client tax preparation.

AFFILIATIONS

Member, Municipal Finance Officers Association of the United States

Member, American Accounting Association

EDUCATION

Bachelor of Business Administration, Hardee College, 1968.

Graduated from West Deerfield Public Schools, 1964.

PERSONAL

Born: July 6, 1946, West Deerfield, Nebraska
Height: 5′ 9″
Weight: 140 lbs.
Status: Married, 2 children
Health: Excellent

References provided on request.

EXAMPLE G

SIDNEY SMITH
0000 Market Street
Milam, Texas 00000
(000) 000-0000

OBJECTIVE

Position in Museum Administration.

CAREER HIGHLIGHTS

Designed and executed exhibition for Teheran Museum.

Have written interpretive summaries of archaelogical data for Smithsonian.

First-hand experience in archaeological sites, both in this country and abroad.

WORK EXPERIENCE

1973–1976	Crew Chief, Tejas Mound Excavation #2, Cherokee County, Texas. Directed crew of ten in dig sponsored by the Smithsonian Institute. Responsible for determining objectives, workload, personnel needs, and equipment requirements. Wrote interpretive summaries of data.
Jan. 1973– May 1973	Member of Smithsonian-sponsored archaeological research team, as part of college semester abroad program, Sungur, Iran. Supervised six Persian workmen. Designed and executed exhibition of findings for Teheran Museum.
1968–1972	Tour Guide, Madison County Museum and County Historical Tour, during summers, holidays, and part-time during college terms, while attending college.

EDUCATION

B.A., Anthropology, 1973, The University of Texas at North Zulch.

Diploma, 1969, Flynn High School, Flynn, Texas.

PERSONAL

Born: December 2, 1951, Flynn, Texas
Status: Single
Health: Excellent

EXAMPLE H

SIDNEY SMITH
1234 Mesquite Street
Los Angeles, California 00000
(000) 000-0000

OBJECTIVE

Position in Museum Administration.

WORK EXPERIENCE

1976–Present	Exhibition Coordinator, Valley Museum of Natural History. Plan special exhibits for the museum, assist in designing and placing exhibits, prepare catalogs and identifying data, and report directly to the Museum Curator.
1973–1976	Crew Chief, Tejas Mound Excavation #2, Cherokee County, Texas. Directed crew of ten in dig sponsored by the Smithsonian Institute. Responsible for determining objectives, workload, personnel needs, and equipment requirements. Wrote interpretive summaries of data.
Jan. 1973– May 1973	Member of Smithsonian-sponsored archaeological research team, as part of college semester abroad programs, Sungur, Iran. Supervised six Persian workmen. Designed and executed exhibition of findings for Teheran Museum.
1968–1972	Tour Guide, Madison County Museum and County Historical Tour, during summers, holidays, and part-time during college terms, while attending University of Texas at North Zulch.

EDUCATION

B.A., Anthropology, 1973, The University of Texas at North Zulch.

Diploma, 1969, Flynn High School, Flynn, Texas.

PERSONAL

Born: December 2, 1951, Flynn, Texas
Status: Single
Health: Excellent

Examples E & F—Chris Jones

Like Helen Marie Smith, Chris Jones drifted into his ultimate career. He came from a pragmatic middle-class family that considered his original goal of becoming a certified public accountant sensible and secure. Through college, his career went routinely, and he was hired immediately after graduation by an accounting firm. Example E, p. 50, shows his first résumé.

However, after only two years at the accounting firm, he was approached for a job by the director of finance for the city where he lived. The work would be little different from what he had been doing at the accounting firm, but there was much more variety, and the possibility of moving up more quickly to a position of greater responsibility.

He accepted the position of budget control under the director of finance. Within two years, his boss retired and he was offered his job. After eight years of successfully running the finances of the city of Pine Valley, he began to consider broader horizons and applied for a similar position in a larger city where he could take night courses in city management. Example F, p. 51, is the résumé he submitted to obtain the job.

Examples G & H—Sidney Smith

Changing positions within related fields can also be intentional. Sidney Smith's move was entirely calculated. Even as a child, Sidney had enjoyed the romance of archaeology and ancient history. By the age of twelve he had amassed a good collection of arrowheads and pottery shards that he found while wandering about the fields and riverbanks near his home.

When he entered college, he knew how impractical it was to dream of being an archaeologist. He planned instead for a career in museum administration.

During his last year of college, he considered himself extremely fortunate to have the opportunity to participate in a Smithsonian-sponsored dig in Iran.

When he was offered a job by the Smithsonian after graduation, working on a site in his home state, he was delighted. The dig lasted three years. At that point, he knew that he could not count on his luck lasting forever. It was time for him to apply for a job in museum administration. Example G, p. 52, is the résumé he submitted.

After four years as an exhibition coordinator, his résumé was extremely impressive. (Example H, p. 53.)

EXAMPLE I

JULIA DOE
111 Lake Drive
Dwight, Colorado 00000
(000) 000-0000

OBJECTIVE

Administrative position in private school. Willing to teach part time.

EXPERIENCE

1970–Present
Teacher

Dwight High School, Dwight, Colorado. Taught American History, World History, and one class of Civics.

1969–1970
Student Teacher

Talbert High School, Talbert, Colorado. Student taught in class of American History.

EDUCATION

M.A., School Administration, 1975; Madison State Teachers College, Madison, Colorado. In addition to regular curriculum, participated in special seminar on "Discipline Problems of the Seventies."

B.A., Education, 1970; Talbert State Teachers College, with emphasis on History. Grade average: 3.9. Graduated Summa Cum Laude.

Diploma, 1966; North Mine High School, North Mine City, Colorado. Class Valedictorian.

AFFILIATIONS

Member, American Federation of Teachers.

Member Rho Rho Rho Sorority.

PERSONAL

Born: April 13, 1948; North Mine City, Colorado.
Status: Married
Health: Excellent

References supplied on request.

EXAMPLE J

JULIA DOE
111 Lake Drive
Dwight, Colorado 00000
(000) 000-0000

OBJECTIVE

Position as School Principal in Private School.

EXPERIENCE

1978–Present Principal	The Dolby School, Dwight, Colorado. Manage office staff of five, with thirty teachers.
1975–1978 Assistant Principal	The Dolby School. Assisted the principal with office duties until her retirement; then assumed her job. In addition to office work, taught two classes of American History.
1970–1975 Teacher	Dwight High School, Dwight, Colorado. Taught American History, World History, and one class of Civics.

EDUCATION

M.A., School Administration, 1976; Madison State Teachers College, Madison, Colorado.

B.A., Education, 1970; Talbert State Teachers College, with emphasis on History. Grade average: 3.9. Graduated Summa Cum Laude. Student taught (1969–1970) in American History, Talbert High School, Talbert, Colorado.

Diploma, 1966; North Mine High School, North Mine City, Colorado. Class Valedictorian.

AFFILIATIONS

Member, American Federation of Teachers.
Member, National Association of School Administrators.

PERSONAL

Born: April 13, 1948; North Mine City, Colorado.
Status: Married
Health: Excellent

References supplied on request.

EXAMPLE K

ASHLEY SMITH
000 East 84th Street
New York, New York 00000
(222) 222-2222

PERSONAL DATA

Age: 25
Height: 5′ 9″
Weight: 105 lbs.
Hair: Blonde
Eyes: Green
Complexion: Fair

Bust: 33″
Waist: 24″
Hips: 34″
Dress Size: 8
Shoe Size: 6
Glove Size: 6

MODELING EXPERIENCE

Fashion Layouts: Vogue, Harper's Bazaar, Mademoiselle

Advertising: L'Interdit (hair), Ladylove Cosmetics (face), New Nails (hands), Skool & Ski Stockings (legs)

Fashion Shows: Paul DuPre Collections
Ciel Cie Furs
Mondriani Sportswear
Fashion on Ice
Donatello Collections

Showroom: Employed as Showroom Model and Mannequin by Paul DuPre (1969–1970).

SPECIAL TALENTS

Ski

Ice Skate

Swim

Dance

Know gymnastics, ballet, and modern dance.

EDUCATION

B.A., Merchandising, New York University, 1969. Courses in Fashion, Management, Merchandising, Product Development, Display, Bookkeeping, and Budgeting.

Brooklyn Public Schools, Brooklyn, New York, 1953–1965.

Portfolio shown by request.

REPRESENTED BY
THE GILLIAN GAY AGENCY
(000) 000-0000

EXAMPLE L

ASHLEY SMITH
0000 East 84th Street
New York, New York 00000
(222) 222-2222

OBJECTIVE

Position with Department Store, utilizing my knowledge of Fashion and Merchandising.

SPECIAL SKILLS

Familiar with the designer fashion market. Know many of the designers personally, and am acquainted with many of their salespersons.

Good judgment of what sells and what doesn't in high fashion market.

Employment

Free-lance
Modeling
(1968–1970)

Represented by the Gillian Gay Agency, began modeling while still a student in college, doing fashion layouts for Vogue, Harper's Bazaar, and Mademoiselle. Have done numerous fashion shows.

Showroom Model
(1969–1970)

Paul DuPre. Modeled in showroom and served as his mannequin for three collections.

EDUCATION

B.A., Merchandising, New York University, 1969. Courses in Fashion, Management, Merchandising, Product Development, Display, Bookkeeping, and Budgeting.

Brooklyn Public Schools, Brooklyn, New York, 1953–1965.

HOBBIES

Skiing, ice skating, gymnastics, dance, and swimming.

PERSONAL

Born: October 12, 1947, Brooklyn, New York
Height: 5′ 9″
Weight: 120 lbs.
Status: Married
Health: Excellent

References furnished on request.

EXAMPLE M

ASHLEY SMITH
0000 East 84th Street
New York, New York 00000
(222) 222-2222

JOB OBJECTIVE

Position as Fashion Buyer with Department Store.

EMPLOYMENT RECORD

1977–Present	<u>Buyer,</u> Designer Sportswear, Henry Taylor & Company, New York. Attended all designer showings and went into the market to select the very best for Henry Taylor's. Restyled the 5th Floor Sportswear department to give it a fresh new look.
1975–1977	<u>Assistant Buyer,</u> Designer Fashions, Marc's Fifth Avenue. Went into the market with the buyer, and assisted in managing the department, taking care of many of the problems of the sales help.
1973–1975	<u>Management Trainee,</u> Marc's Fifth Avenue. Worked in all departments of the store, selling, assisting the buyers and merchandise managers, helping with counter and window displays, and generally learned the approach that gives Marc's Fifth Avenue its fine reputation.
1968–1973	<u>Model,</u> primarily in fashion, with some photographic work for magazines and advertising. Employed as Showroom Model by Paul DuPre (1969–1970).

EDUCATION

B.A., Merchandising, New York University, 1969. Courses in Fashion, Management, Merchandising, Product Development, Display, Bookkeeping, and Budgeting.

Brooklyn Public Schools, Brooklyn, New York, 1953–1965.

PERSONAL

Born: October 12, 1947, Brooklyn, New York
Height: 5′ 9″
Weight: 120 lbs.
Status: Married
Health: Excellent

Examples I & J—Julia Doe

Some job changes require extra effort. Such a case was Julia Doe's. When Julia graduated from college, she wanted to be a teacher. She had no difficulty getting a job teaching high school history.

It took her two years to become disillusioned. Attitudes had changed in public schools since her own high school years. Even the best students were not interested in history, and the discipline problems increased with each year.

She still believed strongly in education, and she wanted to continue her career. After considerable deliberation, she decided she would go into school administration. She returned to college, taking courses at night and during the summers, and obtained her master's degree in School Administration in 1975.

She resigned from her position with the public school, and submitted her résumé (Example I, p. 55) to a private school. She was offered the job of assistant principal with the requirement that she also had to teach. When the principal retired, she was promoted.

Her final résumé is seen in Example J, p. 56.

Examples K, L, and M—Ashley Smith

Careers may take all sorts of odd twists and turns. When Ashley Smith started college, she had no intention of being a fashion model. While she was interested in fashion, her objective was to become a buyer or merchandise manager for a department store. However, she was attractive and had a distinctive look. At a party, while she was still in college, she met a modeling agent who suggested that she might be able to get some part-time modeling work.

Thinking it would be a lark, she accepted. She was attracted to the glamorous world of fashion, and was delighted by her success in it.

It remained part-time work during the rest of her college career, but it became full time after she obtained her degree in merchandising, her original career goal.

For this reason, her first résumé was a modeling résumé. (Example K, p. 57.)

But when she was married, she had to give up this career. Though the life of a model is exciting and glamorous, it is also gruelling and time-consuming. It offered almost no time for a personal life.

Ashley Smith gave up her modeling career and returned to her original plan. In many ways, it seemed a step backward. She had to accept a position as a management trainee with an income considerably lower than her modeling fees. Example L is the résumé she used to get the trainee job.

Seven years later, she had reached the top again. Example M, p. 59, is her résumé as a buyer.

EXAMPLE N

CHARLES DOE
000 West 78th Street
New York, New York 00000
(000) 000-0000

Member: AEA   SAG   AFTRA

Height: 6′
Weight: 165 lbs.

Hair: Brown

Eyes: Brown

Agent: Bill Smith

000 West 42nd St.

New York, N.Y. 00000
(000) 000-0000

THEATER

Broadway: Asa Jones, *Harper's Ferry* (1966)

Off-Broadway: Henry, *The Dog Who Laughed* (1967)
Clown, *Circus Freaks* (1965)

Off-Off: Mehitabel, *The Bible Revised* (1968), Tavern Theater
Featured in *The Lost Review* (1965), Tavern Theater
The Boy, *Sex and the Singular Boy* (1969), Young Poets Theater
Jerry Cracker, *Hunks I Have Known* (1970), The Preposterous
Workshop

The New Jersey Shakespeare Festival: Young Siward, *Macbeth* (1971); Young
Cato, *Julius Caesar* (1972); Peter Quince, *A Midsummer Night's Dream*
(1973)

FILM

Public Television: Marco Polo, *The Explorers* (1974)
Richard Henry Lee, *The Lee Chronicles* (1975)

COMMERCIALS

STUD After Shave (1971); GREGOR Beer (1972); ACTIVE Jeans (1973)

TRAINING

Voice: Dick Doe, Caroline Jones
Acting: Roger Reed, Lawrence Lee
Mime: Pierre Pliet

B.F.A., Drama, Chicago City University, 1965. Studied Acting, Voice, Dance &
Movement, Improvisation, Directing. Appeared in six productions, playing
the lead in two, performing supporting roles in three, and appearing as a
featured actor in one.

EXAMPLE O

CHARLES DOE
000 West 78th Street
New York, New York 00000
(000) 000-0000

JOB OBJECTIVE

Position as Data Analyst with Information Processing Company.

WORK EXPERIENCE

Data Analyst	Information Unlimited (1977–Present). Set up and interpreted special programs for clients, using a wide range of formats—economic, geographical, political, ethnic, educational, etc.
Computer Programmer	Information Unlimited (1971–1977). Using both IBM 360 and FORTRAN IV, programmed data, supervised other programmers, and helped to train new employees.
Programmer Trainee	Information Unlimited (1967–1971). Learned programming on the job.
Toby Office Temps	Did temporary clerical work for a variety of businesses and firms (1965–1966).

EDUCATION

Chicago City University, B.F.A., 1965.

Branch Creek Public Schools, Branch Creek, Illinois, 1949–1961.

HOBBIES AND INTERESTS

Read extensively on all subjects. Enjoy writing, the theater, and music. Play tennis and softball.

PERSONAL

Born: July 28, 1943, Branch Creek, Illinois
Status: Married, 1 child
Health: Excellent

References provided on request.

Examples N and O—Charles Doe

Charles Doe also had to give up his goal of a glamorous career for something more pragmatic, but his career took a path different from Ashley Smith's.

He intended to have a career as an actor. He had the looks and talent, and for a while he had the luck necessary for success.

Acting is one of the riskiest of careers; at least in the beginning, actors need a second job that will pay their way while they struggle to get acting work. When Charles Doe first arrived in New York, he took jobs through a temporary agency and fit in other work between casting calls.

Within two months, he was cast in an off-Broadway play, and by the end of a year he was on Broadway. But that proved to be the height of his acting career. The next year, he got another part in an off-Broadway play. After that, he was turned down for one part after another.

It took him a while to realize the reason. In the late sixties, theater was changing. Good-looking actors were out, and ordinary or ugly actors were in. Except for Shakespearean productions, the only work he could get was in nonpaying off-off-Broadway productions, in which he had to remove part or all of his clothing.

However, his luck did not leave him entirely. It was sheer luck that started him on his second career. A computer programming firm, Information Unlimited, was just getting started. Because they did not know from one week to the next how large a staff they would need for the work on hand, they chose to hire aspiring actors and actresses on an "on call" basis, and train them in computer programming.

Charles Doe was one of their more regular workers, and, as it turned out, one of their better ones. He had a talent for numbers and statistics.

For several years he continued to concentrate on his acting career. In 1974 and 1975, he managed to get work in two public television films, and he was optimistic enough to get married. Meanwhile, he was doing supervisory work at Information Unlimited.

But after 1975, he was getting more modeling work than acting jobs. Example N, p. 61, is his acting résumé in 1975.

The next year his first child was born and he had to reassess his prospects. By 1977, when he was promoted to full-time data analyst at Information Unlimited, he had given up his acting career.

Example O is his data analyst résumé in 1980. In looking at it, one has to strain to see that he ever had any other career goal in mind.

EXAMPLE P

PAUL JONES
123 West Elm Street
Birchdale, Connecticut 00000
(000) 000-0000

OBJECTIVE

Editorial position with magazine.

EXPERIENCE

Editor-in-Chief,
1971–1975

Harrow's Monthly magazine. Set editorial policy, supervised editorial staff, wrote monthly column "The Editor's Desk," and special articles from time to time.

Associate Editor,
1968–1971

Harrow's Monthly magazine. Assigned and edited articles written by free-lance writers, wrote one article for each issue, and participated in editorial meetings.

Staff Writer,
1965–1968

Continent magazine. Wrote articles on assignment, at least one per issue. Assisted in photo research, and did some editing and rewriting of articles submitted from free-lance writers.

EDUCATION

B.A., Journalism, Ohio Eastern University, 1965.

Graduated, McLane High School, McLane Ohio, 1961. Attended McLane Public Schools, 1949–1961.

ACTIVITIES AND HONORS

Phi Beta Kappa
Member, Sigma Delta Chi
Brown Literary Award and Scholarship
Editor-in-Chief, *Ariadne*, student literary magazine, 1964–65. Wrote articles 1962–1965.
Contributed articles to *Continent* magazine concerning Civil Rights Movement and Student Activism, 1963–1965.

PERSONAL

Born: May 13, 1943, Cincinnati, Ohio
Status: Married, 2 children
Health: Excellent

EXAMPLE Q

PAUL JONES
123 West Elm Street
Birchdale, Connecticut 00000
(000) 000-0000

FREE-LANCE WRITER

Available For:

Book and Magazine Assignments * Advertising Copy * Press Releases * Book Jacket Copy * Record Liner Notes

---

CREDITS

Books: Don't Speak to Your Plants, until Spoken To (1977)
Don't Eat Anything You Don't Want Repeated (1979)
The Too-Short History of the American Magazine (1978, with John Smith)

Articles: "The Decline of the American Presidency" (Continent magazine), "Too Late to Stop the Holocaust?" (Continent magazine), "Grow Your Own Food Indoors" (Table Talk magazine), "Making Do with Smaller Dollars" (The Monthly Review), and numerous others.

Liner Notes: For Classical Motion Picture Soundtrack, and Broadway Show Albums—Town Records.

Book Jacket Copy: For both Fiction and Nonfiction—Downing House, Inc., and Bright & Brown.

EMPLOYMENT

1971–1975   Editor-in-Chief, Harrow's Monthly magazine.

1968–1971   Associate Editor, Harrow's Monthly magazine.

1965–1968   Staff Writer, Continent magazine.

EDUCATION

B.A., Journalism, Ohio Eastern University, 1965.

PERSONAL

Born: May 13, 1943, Cincinnati, Ohio
Status: Married, but free to travel on assignment
Health: Excellent
Spoken Languages: French, Spanish, Italian

EXAMPLE R

MILTON DOE
0000 Hackberry Blvd.
Beach City, New Jersey 00000
(111) 111-1111

JOB OBJECTIVE

Position as chemist with industrial firm.

EDUCATION

Presently attending night school, East New Jersey State College, with goal of obtaining M.S. degree in Chemistry. As of June 1976, have 12 points toward degree.

1973, B.A. in Education, with emphasis on Chemistry, East New Jersey State College.

1968, Diploma from Beach City High School. Attended Beach City Public Schools, 1956–1968.

EXPERIENCE

1973–1976	Chemistry Teacher, Beach City High School. In addition to three classes of Chemistry, taught one class of General Science each semester, and served as Assistant Coach for the school basketball team.
1969–1973	Shipping Clerk, night shift, Brolax Company. Worked in warehouse while attending college.
Summer 1967	Drove fork-lift, Brolax Company warehouse.
Summer 1965	Road crew, New Jersey Highway Department.

HOBBIES AND ACTIVITIES

Refinishing and restoring antique furniture.

Photography.

PERSONAL

Born: August 8, 1950; Beach City, New Jersey
Height: 6′ 1″
Weight: 180 lbs.
Status Married, 1 child
Health: Excellent

References provided on request.

EXAMPLE S

MILTON DOE
0000 Hackberry Blvd.
Beach City, New Jersey 00000
(111) 111-1111

JOB OBJECTIVE

Position as chemist with industrial firm.

EXPERIENCE

1976–Present	Chemist, Brolax Company, Beach City, N.J. Supervise production of Brolax Liquid and Brolax Powder, testing for consistency of chemical content.
1973–1976	Chemistry Teacher, Beach City High School. In addition to three classes of Chemistry, taught one class of General Science each semester, and served as Assistant Coach for the school basketball team.
1969–1973	Shipping Clerk, night shift, Brolax Company. Worked in warehouse while attending college.

EDUCATION

1978, M.S. in Chemistry, East New Jersey State College. Attended night school, 1975–1978.

1973, B.A. in Education, with emphasis on Chemistry, East New Jersey State College.

1968, Diploma from Beach City High School. Attended Beach City Public Schools, 1956–1968.

HOBBIES AND ACTIVITIES

Coach Little League Baseball team.

Refinishing and restoring antique furniture.

Photography.

PERSONAL

Born: August 8, 1950; Beach City, New Jersey
Height: 6′ 1″
Weight: 180 lbs.
Status: Married, 1 child
Health: Excellent

EXAMPLE T

FRANCES JONES
0000 Third Avenue
New York, New York 00000
(222) 222-2222

JOB OBJECTIVE

Position as Secretary with Book Editor.

SKILLS AND TALENTS

Type 70 words per minute; take dictation 70 words per minute.

Familiar with editing and proofreading symbols.

Know how to operate dictaphone.

Good telephone voice.

Eager to learn about book publishing.

EDUCATION

B.A., English, 1968, New York University; 3.5 grade average. Special emphasis on American literature. Participated in Seminar in Book Publishing, 1966.

Diploma, The Hilton School, New York, 1964; ranked third in class.

Martin's Secretarial School, 1968; night classes in typing and shorthand.

HOBBIES AND ACTIVITIES

Since second year in college have been writing articles for magazines. "Colleges in Crisis" published in *Continent* magazine, 1966. "American Students Build a Bridge to Turkey" published in *World* magazine, 1967. "What Students Teach the Teachers" published in *New Educator* magazine, 1968.

Student Summer Work Program, Eregli, Turkey, Summer 1967. One of twelve American students selected to work with twelve Turkish students to rebuild a bridge.

PERSONAL

Born: November 20, 1946; New York City
Status: Single
Health: Excellent

EXAMPLE U

FRANCES JONES
0000 Third Avenue
New York, New York 00000
(222) 222-2222

JOB OBJECTIVE

Position as Editor with Trade Book Publisher

EXPERIENCE

1976–Present	Senior Editor, Silver House Books, Inc.: Responsible for series of books on crafts, home repair, and other "how to" subjects. Published several successful diet and health titles.
1973–1976	Editor, Eberhart, Conklin, & Matthews, Inc.: Assumed list of cookbooks from previous editor, and developed a line of health, diet, and beauty books.
1970–1973	Administrative Assistant to Editor-in-chief, Eberhart, Conklin, & Matthews, Inc.: Helped to coordinate work of various editors and staff. Assisted editor-in-chief in various editorial matters, including taking responsibility for unsolicited manuscripts.
1968–1970	Editorial Secretary, Sullivan & Sullivan, Inc.: All typing and filing for two editors.

EDUCATION

B.A., English, 1968, New York University; 3.5 grade average.

Diploma, The Hilton School, New York, 1964; ranked third in class.

Martin's Secretarial School, 1968; night classes in typing and shorthand.

HOBBIES AND ACTIVITIES

Since second year in college have been writing articles for magazines; twelve have been published.

Student Summer Work Program, Eregli, Turkey, Summer 1967.

PERSONAL

Born: November 20, 1946; New York City.
Status: Single
Health: Excellent

Examples P & Q—Paul Jones

Paul Jones was also forced by circumstances—or luck—to change his career after a number of years.

He was a highly successful magazine editor in 1975 when the recession hit, and the magazine for which he was editor-in-chief folded. He was married with two children, and his family was accustomed to living in an affluent style since his income had been rather high.

As soon as *Harrow's Monthly* closed its doors, Paul prepared a résumé (Example P, p. 64), and set out in search of work. There were no jobs available at his level; when he expressed a willingness to accept something less, employers were skeptical. (It is easier to make a résumé look more impressive than it is to make one look less impressive.)

Paul Jones finally had to face the prospect of changing his career. The only alternative he could see was to become a free-lance writer. At first, he took assignments from magazines, then he came up with a few book ideas.

Very quickly he found himself successful at his second career. Example Q is his free-lance writer résumé for 1980.

Examples R & S—Milton Doe

Milton Doe also changed his career for economic reasons, but he made the change by choice. Like Julia Doe, he wanted to be a teacher. However, he had to work very hard to get his college degree and teaching certificate. His family could not pay his college expenses, and so he had to pay his own way by working summers and nights while going to school.

He succeeded in getting what he wanted, only to discover it had not been worth the effort. Although he had a high regard for knowledge and a great respect for work, like Julia Doe, he was disappointed in student attitudes. His students did not have the incen-

tive he had as a young man to learn and to get ahead in life.

He had a wife and a child to support, and his teaching salary was just barely enough for them to make ends meet. He did not like the idea that his wife and child had to suffer for his idealism, especially when his idealism was not producing results.

He went back to school in the evenings, obtained a master's degree in chemistry (the subject he taught), and applied for work with a chemical company. The résumé he submitted is Example R, p. 66. After four years with the chemical company, he prepared Example S, p. 67, to get an even better paying job.

Examples T & U—Frances Jones

Frances Jones planned the changes and steps in her career quite methodically. She wanted to be an editor. Her parents had friends in publishing, and she asked for their advice when she was still in high school. She was disappointed to learn that there was no clear-cut method for becoming an editor, especially for a woman.

However, they recommended that she get the best education she could and learn as much as possible about books and writing. Then she might squeeze in through the side door as an editorial secretary or as a copy editor. They warned her that copy-editing could prove to be a dead-end job.

Frances decided to risk the secretarial route. During her last year of college, she took night courses at a secretarial school. After graduation, she set out to get her first job using the résumé in Example T, p. 68.

She got a position as editorial secretary, and gave herself two years to become an assistant to an editor. She didn't manage it with the first publisher, and so made a move to one where the prospects were better.

Within another three years, she was an editor. Example U, p. 69, is her résumé after seven years as editor.

EXAMPLE V

MARGE SMITH
1234 North Memphis Street
Nashville, Tennessee 00000
(000) 000-0000

OBJECTIVE

Secretarial position.

SKILLS

Type 75 words per minute on IBM Electric, no errors.

Type 60 words per minute on Office Standard, no errors.

Take shorthand, 80 words per minute.

Operate Dictaphone dictation machine.

Know filing systems and some bookkeeping procedures.

Familiar with most legal terminology.

EDUCATION

South Nashville Secretarial School (1972–1973); learned typing, shorthand, and clerical procedures.

East Arkansas University (1968–1970), majoring in music.

Graduated from Ashley High School, 1968, Ashley, Arkansas. Attended Ashley Public Schools (1956–1968).

HOBBIES AND ACTIVITIES

Play piano, organ, and guitar.

Attend concerts.

Member of Executive Board of The New World Community (1970–1973). Authored covenant, dealt with lawyer, and served as secretary.

As part of Student YWCA program, worked with migrant workers, Summer 1969, improving housing conditions.

PERSONAL

Born: February 4, 1950; Ashley, Arkansas
Status: Single
Height: 5′ 5″
Weight: 95 lbs.
Health: Excellent

71

EXAMPLE W

MARGE SMITH
1234 North Memphis Street
Nashville, Tennessee 00000
(000) 000-0000

OBJECTIVE

Position as Secretary or Assistant to Record Producer.

SKILLS AND TALENTS

Familiar with lifestyles of rock and country musicians.

Know recording contracts, and understand royalties.

Typing speed: 75 words per minute.

Shorthand speed: 80 words per minute.

EXPERIENCE

Secretary, Golden Bee Records (1973–1974). Secretary to head of royalty department. Typed contracts and royalty statements, and heavily involved with answering royalty and contract questions from agents and artists.

EDUCATION

South Nashville Secretarial School (1972–1973); learned typing, shorthand, and clerical procedures.

East Arkansas University (1968–1970), majoring in music.

Graduated from Ashley High School, 1968, Ashley, Arkansas.

HOBBIES AND ACTIVITIES

Play piano, organ, and guitar; and attend concerts.

Member of Executive Board of the New World Community (1970–1973).

Worked with migrant workers, Summer 1969.

PERSONAL

Born: February 4, 1950; Ashley, Arkansas
Status: Single
Height: 5′ 5″
Weight: 95 lbs.
Health: Excellent

EXAMPLE X

MARGE SMITH
1234 North Memphis Street
Nashville, Tennessee 00000
(000) 000-0000

OBJECTIVE

Position as Record Producer with recording company.

EXPERIENCE

Producer | Dirt-Dauber Records (1977–Present). Produced all major albums by the Spikes, Annabelle Lee, and The Two Tones. Also developed a new sound for The Feint-Hearts. Worked closely with the promotion department and with the design department on jacket covers.

Administrative Assistant | Dirt-Dauber Records (1976–1977). Assistant to producer Bill Jones, performing functions of secretary as well. Managed office, wrote liner notes, arranged recording dates and conferences, prepared contracts.

Secretary | Golden Bee Records (1973–1974). Secretary to head of royalty department. Involved heavily with answering royalty and contract questions from agents and artists.

EDUCATION

East Arkansas University (1968–1970), majored in music.

South Nashville Secretarial School (1972–1973); learned typing, shorthand, and clerical procedures.

Graduated from Ashley High School, 1968, Ashley, Arkansas.

PERSONAL

Born: February 4, 1950; Ashley, Arkansas
Status: Single
Health: Excellent

References provided on request.

Examples V, W, and X—Marge Smith

With her early handicaps, one would never have expected Marge Smith to have a highly successful career, but she did it, and much credit should go to her résumés.

Like Frances Jones, her first job was secretarial, but there the similarity between them ends.

Marge Smith was in her second year of college, majoring in music, when she dropped out to join a commune at the crest of the counter-culture movement.

The commune managed to stay together only two-and-a-half years, and Marge found herself ill qualified to enter the job market. Her relationship with her parents was strained, but she persuaded them to foot the bill for secretarial school.

She knew it would require an exceptional employer to hire her, even if she minimized her commune experience. When she submitted the résumé in Example V, p. 71, she focused on the recording industry, a field in which she felt she could be frank about her accomplishments in the commune.

She had no difficulty getting a secretarial job. However, she held the job for only two years. When a rock musician asked her to join him on the road, she willingly became a "groupie."

Two years later they split. She was on her own again, looking for work, and without a very good job record. She did not want to take a step backward again, and she realized she had learned some things in her two years with the musician. She had become familiar with the lifestyles of rock and country performers, and she could talk their language.

This time, she aimed a bit higher than secretary, figuring she had nothing to lose. Using the résumé in Example W, p. 72, she got a job as administrative assistant to a record producer.

Within two years, she was producing records herself. Her final résumé as a record producer is seen in Example X, p. 73.

Index

Index

N

Negative qualities, avoidance of, 7, 9, 10
Newspaper ads, answering with a résumé, 34–35

O

Objective, *see* Job objective section
Objectivity, need for, 14–15
Organizations, membership in, inclusion in résumé, 24
Outlook, positive, importance of, 9

P

Personal approach, résumés and the, 36
Personal data section (résumé), 16, 21, 26–27, 31
Personnel agencies, 35–36
Phone number, inclusion in résumé, 16
Photocopying (résumés), 31
Physical handicaps, résumés and, 27
Positive outlook, importance of, 9
Positive qualities, emphasizing, 7–10
Preliminary résumé, 10–15 examples of, 11–13
Preparation of résumés, 9
Previous employment section (résumé), *see* Work experience section
Principal, school, résumé for job as, 56, 60
Problems, résumé, dealing with, 7, 44–73
Professional affiliations section (résumé), 16, 24
Punctuality, importance of, 9

Q

Qualifications, specific, looked for by employers, 9
Qualities
  looked for by employers, 9
  negative, avoidance of, 7, 9, 10
  positive, emphasizing, 7–10

R

Reasons for leaving previous jobs, 9
Record producer, résumé for job as, 73
References, résumés and, 26, 27
Regulations, attitude toward, 10
Rehearsal, interview, 39–40
Reliability, importance of, 9
Résumé(s)
  answering want ads with, 34–35
  appearance of, 15, 27–31
  bad, 14
    examples of, 11–13
  blind approach in mailing out, 32–34
  categories in, 16
  confessional, 14, 15, 21
  copies of, 31, 40
  education section, 12, 13, 24, 31
  format of, 15–16, 19, 28
  functions of, 15
  hobbies section, 12, 24, 26
  identifying data section, 16, 28
  importance of, 8
  interviews and, 8, 40
  job objective section, 11, 13, 16–17, 21, 28
  military record section, 16, 24, 31
  personal approach and, 36
  personal data section, 16, 21, 26–27, 31